ALL THE POPES

FROM SAINT PETER TO FRANCIS

Lozzi Roma
edizioni turistiche

INTRODUCTION

The word Pope derives from the ancient Greek word pàppas (father) which refers to the spiritual paternity of bishops. The term was first used in the Orient, it was not used in the West until the first half of the 5th century. It was affirmed definitively in the 8th century as the official title for the Bishop of Rome, the successor of the Apostle Peter. In the hierarchy of the church, the word pontiff has the same meaning.

Since 1059, the election of the Pope has been entrusted exclusively to the Church cardinals to limit interference from external political influences. The figure of universality prevails definitively on the Rome Bishop and reinforces the role of monarch. Since the first half of the 13th century the Pope has defined the doctrinal development of concepts such as the vicarious cristi, which is the foundation for the belief that the Pope, with his sacred investiture, is above humanity. The First Vatican Council (1870) deemed the Pope infallible in a moral and doctrinal sense, with the definition ex cathedra.

The new "Universal Church Calendar" no longer lists all of the first 54 popes as saints; for clarity and respect of the time-worn tradition which considered them so, the title (Saint) is written in parenthesis for the popes that are no longer considered as such.

The mosaic medallion icons are reproductions of the busts of the popes, which can be found on Via Ostiense at the Basilica of Saint Paul's Outside the Walls in Rome. Each circle, reproduced on models by the Vatican School, is 1.90 meters in diameter with a frame of gilded bronze.

The habit of adopting a Pontifical Stem was introduced by Pope Innocent III and has continued without interruption. Generally, popes with nobile origins used their family stem. The tradition continues today and even popes without nobile origins have adopted a sSem, usually based on a personal choice or particular devotion (such as the Virgin Mary on the papal Stem of John Paul II). It is usually used on all official documents signed by the Sainted Father including enclyclicals, papal bulls, as well as works.

For chronologically ordering the 266 Pontifical Heads of the Church, we scrupulously followed the Annuals of the Vatican Pontificate. For further clarification, take note that of the 266 popes considered (264 to be exact, because Benedict IX was elected three times during the tremendous battles between popes and antipopes during the medieval period). Of all the popes, 207 are Italian and 106 are Roman. The number of antipopes has been definitively set at 37. With the term antipope, we intend an antagonist elected irregularly alongside the legitimate Pope.

There have been 57 non-Italian popes, of the following nationalities: 19 French, 14 Greek, 8 Syrian, 6 German, 3 African, 2 Spanish, 1 Austrian, 1 Portuguese, 1 Palestinian, 1 English, 1 Dutch, 1 Polish and 1 Argentine Pope.

"ALL THE POPES from Saint Peter to Francis"
© LOZZI ROMA s.a.s.
ISBN 978-88-6838-032-8

LOZZI ROMA S.a.s.
Via R. Rodriguez Pereira, 102/a - 00136 Rome
Tel. (+39) 06 35497051 / 06 97841668
info@lozziroma.com
www.lozziroma.it

Printed by:
Press Up srl - www.pressup.it

Photographs:
© Servizio fotografico de L'Osservatore Romano.
© Basilica of St. Paul's Outside the Walls - Rome.
© Archivio fotografico Lozzi Roma.
Made in Italy
www.gruppolozzi.it

A SHORT HISTORY OF THE PAPACY

The title "Pope" was originally bestowed on all bishops, but since the 5th century it has been reserved exclusively for the Bishop of Rome. In the Roman Catholic Church, the Pope has the power of divine institution, because he is the Vicar of Christ and the successor of Saint Peter to whom Christ entrusted the duty of perpetuating his Word "until the end of time."

The authority of the Bishop of Rome was affirmed between the 1st and 4th century. The first known Pontifical Act dates back to the year 96 and was issued by Saint Clement to the Christian community in Corinth. In the 2nd century the Bishop of Carthage, Saint Cyprian, defined the Roman Church as "the central Church from which the unity of the clergy springs." More explicit acknowledgement of Christianity's diffusion throughout the Roman Empire came about with the edict of Milan (313), issued by Emperor Constantine, allowing Christians religious freedom and restoring possessions that had been confiscated from them. Furthermore, the Emperor, for religious vocation and to stabilise the empire, took an active role in ecclesiastical organisation. He nominated bishops in many major cities and is responsible for the construction of several Basilicas, including the ancient Saint Peter's Basilica in the Vatican. He is also credited with calling the Nicene Council (325), the first of 22 Ecumenical councils. At the event, 220 bishops reunited and drew up the Nicene Creed or *symbol*, outlining Christian doctrine.

Under the reigns of Constantine and Theodosius (who proclaimed Christianity as the state religion) the temporal power of the Church grew, thanks to gifts from wealthy followers. Saint Sergius affirmed in 385 that the law of the Roman Church was valid everywhere, while the Council of Calcedonia (451) affirmed that "Peter hath spoken by the mouth of the Pope".

At the fall of the Roman Empire in 476, the papacy remained the only power capable of defending the Italian peninsula from the invading barbarians. The pontificate of Saint Leo the Great (440-461) and Saint Gregory the Great (590-604) strengthened the relationship with the new rulers and began the work of spreading Christianity throughout Europe.

Longobard King Liutprando donated Sutri (north of Rome) in 728, to the Church marking the beginnings of the Pontifical State. In the year 755, French King Pepin the Short made ulterior donations following his march into the Italian peninsula to defend Pope Stephen II during the Longobard invasion. French influence reached its apex during the year 800 when Charlemagne was crowned Emperor of the Holy Roman Empire by Pope Saint Leo III.

The decay of the Carolignian Empire (903) and the rise of feudalism weakened the Church immensely. Rome lived through years of siege and battle, which inevitably took its toll on papal power; the period was characterised by weak popes who were at the mercy of stronger factions.

Leo IX presided over The council of Reims in 1049, declaring the Rome Bishop as the First Apostle of the universal Church. The Empire's dominance over the Church waned with Nicholas II. He restored the cardinals' right to elect the Pope in 1059. With the famous humiliation of Emperor Henry IV at Canossa (1077) and the edict of Worms (1122) the papacy gained a dominant role in the exercise of spiritual power throughout Europe. Pope Gregory VII (1073-1085) affirmed papal supremacy with his document *Dictatus Papae,* securing the pontifical right to dismiss the emperor. In the 13th century, Pope Innocent III elaborated the theory of "papal theocracy," awarding the Pope spiritual and temporal power. Emperors, whose powers descended directly by divine will, still did not have enough strength to rule without investiture from the Roman Church. The Pope required an act of obedience from nominated bishops and his delegates were present in churches throughout the European continent to ensure that his decrees were carried out.

The crusades, which began in 1095 under the reign of Urban II, fit perfectly in this context. With Islam occupying the Holy Land, the kingdom united under the symbol of the Holy Cross fighting against a common enemy, which kept feudal contrasts under control.

At the end of the 13th century, the birth of national States (France and England first) and monarchical absolutism, threatened the unity of the Holy Roman Empire and cut deeply into the foundations of pontifical power. French Pope Clement V was pressured by the King of France in 1309 to move the pontifical seat to the city of Avignon in Provence, beginning the "Avignon captivity," which lasted until 1377. During this time the popes were under the tutelage of the King of France. This was followed by the clamorous era of the great Western schism (1378-1417) when two and three popes simultaneously sought the pontifical throne, bringing about heretical and schismatic currents in central Europe.

During the Renaissance (the second half of the 15th century), the Church neglected its spiritual and doctrinal role and fell into merely exercising power. The Pope's hegemonic power ebbed and local discontentment grew, bringing about the rebellion of Luther and Calvin in 1517, which blossomed into the Protestant Reformation. Paul III tried to halt the disintegration of Europe, in 1545, with the council of Trent, which lasted, with various interruptions, until 1563. This resulted in strengthening the papacy and brought about the founding of governing organisations such as the Sant'Uffizio, the Index and new congregations.

During the 17th and 18th century, the curia became very Italian and only Italian popes were nominated until 1978. The affirmation of the large European states brought about a drastic reduction of Papal power, even in Catholic countries.

The French Revolution, in 1789, caught the Sainted Seat completely unprepared to affront the far-reaching issues it caused. Napoleon's imperial ambitions partially restored the Church's political role, in 1804, when the Pope crowned him emperor in Notre Dame. The French conquest of Rome in 1809 and the arrest of Pope Pious VII brought about a long period of pontifical detention that would last until 1813.

After the Vienna Congress (1814-1815), the restoration following Napoleon's reign restored temporal power to the Roman Church and the pontifical state (which extended throughout central Italy) and confirmed the role of spiritual leader to the main governing nobility of Europe. However in the 18th century, the difficulty of managing these two roles kept the Pope from truly understanding the Risorgimento that pervaded the Italian peninsula as well as the central Catholic Hapsburg Empire. The encyclicals published by Gregory XVI and Pius IX against the liberal ideas of the times were written in this context.

The disbanding of the Pontifical State (1870) following the unity of Italy caused the difficult "Roman question" between the Pope and the kingdom of Italy, bringing about the end of the pontificate's temporal power. The voluntary exile of Pius IX, in the Vatican, reshaped the role of the Church in Italy and world politics and limited its power to the sphere of religious doctrine. From that came the first Vatican council's (1870) proclamation of the dogma of papal infallibility and the encyclicals by Leo XIII and Pius X.

Pope Benedict XV (1914-1922) tried, without luck, to convince international communities to desist with the "useless destruction" of the World War I. He did however lay the foundations for the pacifistic policy that has characterised the Church throughout the 20th century.

Pope Pius XI (1922-1939) reached an agreement with the Italian government, led by Mussolini, with the Lateran Pacts (1929), which gave the Church dominion over Vatican City (44 hectares inside the city of Rome) as well as acknowledging Church autonomy in ecclesi-astical organisations throughout the Italian territory. World War II and the difficult times following it characterised the pontificate of Pius XII (1939-1958), who wisely opposed the totalitarian, Nazi and Fascist regimes and was a strong enemy of Soviet Russia. He provided the faithful with conservative doctrine to oppose the rapid changes in world society after the war. Pope John XXIII understood that the Church, in order to maintain an important role in society, had to modernise and to change its institutions to fit the necessities of the modern world. After three years of preparation, in 1962 he called the second Vatican council, which would be continued by Paul VI, and which, left a strong mark on Catholic history, determining the organisation of ecclesiastical structures and the fundamental doctrines that characterise today's Church. In 1978, after the short pontificate of John Paul I (August-September), the conclave of cardinals elected Polish Cardinal Karol Wojtyla as Pope. He took the name John Paul II and during his 27-year pontificate, restored the papacy's importance in political and social issues, accelerating the fall of soviet communism and changing the world's political geography. Following the outline of second Vatican council, Pope Wojtyla fixed several points of religious doctrine and reinforced the Catholic world community's bonds with the Sainted Seat, opening dialogue with other religions, and fighting to stop political conflicts from turning into religious wars.

In April 2005, following the trend, another non-Italian Pope was elected. The German Cardinal Ratzinger, took the name Benedict XVI as Pope. The Pope, during his eight years of pontificate, has noted with dismay a "Church with a disfigured, scarred, torn face, due to the errors of its children, from the simple faithful to the bishops and cardinals". He has also fought, with courage and determination, for the recognition of religious freedom in the world. On 11 February 2013, during the Consistory, Benedict XVI announced his historic and moving resignation: his abdication from "the ministry of the Bishop of Rome, successor of St. Peter, entrusted to me by the hand of the Cardinals April 19, 2005". On 28 February 2013, Benedict XVI left the Vatican by helicopter and moved temporarily into the papal summer residence of Castel Gandolfo.

On the evening of 13 March 2013, on the fifth ballot, Jorge Mario Bergoglio was elected Pope and took the name of Francis in honour of St. Francis of Assisi.

Peter's 266th successor, he presents himself as a humble shepherd, capable of looking at a universal Church that spreads "the announcement of God's love and mercy" everywhere, bringing his style as an energetic and capable Bishop and preacher to the Vatican.

1 – **Saint PETER** (67). He was born in Betsaida. After the Resurrection, on Lake Tiberiade, Christ entrusted his flock, to Peter, consecrating him as pontiff. One of the Twelve Apostles, his name was originally Simon, but was changed by Jesus to Kefa, meaning "rock." Peter was the first of the disciples to whom the Messiah appeared after his resurrection and the first to perform a miracle. He is accredited with the first ecclesiastic ordination, thus he is considered the founder of the Holy Roman Church. Arrested and martyred during Nero's reign, he was crucified head down. He died on June 29, 67 and was buried on Vatican hill, where the Basilica of Saint Peter's now stands.

2 – **(Saint) LINUS** (67-76). Born in Volterra (in the Italian province of Pisa), there is not much information about his life. He was made Pope in 67 and lived through the reigns of five different emperors: Nero, Galba, Otone, Vitellius, and Vespasian. During his pontificate, the Evangelists Mark and Luke were martyred. He is attributed with issuing a decree requiring women to cover their heads when entering sacred places and during religious functions. During this era, the heresies of the Cerinians and the Gnostics took place. Linus was martyred during the reign of Vespasian and was buried next to Saint Peter.

3 – **(Saint) ANACLETUS** (1st century). He was born in Athens. The precise dates are unknown, but presumably his pontificate lasted from 77 until 88. During that time, Emperor Domitian relentlessly persecuted the Christians because they did not want to contribute to restoring the Temple of Jupiter.
Anacletus instituted the first parochial divisions in Rome, separating the city into 25 zones, each directed by a different priest. He was martyred after having a temple built on Saint Peter's tomb, destined as a resting place for martyrs, this is where he was later buried.

4 – **Saint CLEMENT I** (88-97). Born in Rome, he was Peter and Paul's disciple. Martyred during the reign of Emperor Trajan, he was exiled to Turkey and condemned to forced labor. After refusing to make a sacrifice to the gods, in 97, Clement was punished with an atrocious death: he was thrown into the sea with an anchor tied around his neck.
Several written works are attributed to him, nearly all of them are considered apocryphal, except for his *"First letter to the Corinthians,"* which was written in Greek. He is buried in Rome in the Church that carries his name.

5 – **Saint EVARISTUS** (97-105). Originally from Judea, the fourth successor of Peter was elected during the reign of Emperor Trajan. There is not a lot known about his life. It is said that he instituted parochial districts to accommodate the growing numbers of faithful and that he divided the city into diaconates. Each area was entrusted to an older priest, who supervised the diffusion of Christian aid and charity, giving rise to the present day cardinals. The circumstances of his death are unsure, and it is not clear if he was martyred. Neapolitan legend holds that he is buried in Naples in the Church of Saint Mary Major.

6 – **Saint ALEXANDER I** (105-115). Born in Rome, he was a disciple of Plutarch, and the first Pope to be elected by selection of the bishops in Rome instead of the Last Will and Testament of his predecessor.

The third persecution by Emperor Trajan took place during his pontificate.

He is accredited with beginning the tradition of keeping holy water in churches and houses. Alexander was also responsible for the ruling that consecrated communion be made exclusively from unleavened bread. He was probably buried in the Roman Church Santa Sabina.

7 – **(Saint) SIXTUS I** (115-125). Of Roman origin, he was elected Pope during the reign of Emperor Hadrian, who had a tolerant attitude towards the Christians; Sixtus fought against the Gnostic heresy.

He issued many liturgical and disciplinary decrees, such as the provision that the chalice and the paten can only touched by a priest. Pope Sixtus I is also responsible for the introduction of the brief liturgical inno, "*Sanctus*," into the Holy Mass. Probably martyred, it is likely that his sepulchre is in the Cathedral of Alatri and not in the Vatican, which was previously believed to be his final resting place.

8 – **(Saint) TELESPHORUS** (125-136). Of Greek origin, he is remembered for his propensity towards the Eastern tradition of celebrating Easter on a different day than the one adopted in Rome. He composed the inno, "*Gloria in excelsis Deo*," but he is erroneously attributed with the introduction of midnight mass at Christmas time. Venerated as a martyr, his final resting place is unknown, but legend holds that he is buried next to Saint Peter's tomb. Saint Ireneo wrote in "*Historia Ecclesiastica*," that Telesphorus "suffered martyrship gloriously."

9 – **(Saint) HYGINUS** (136-140). Originally from Athens, he was the son of a philosopher and a philosopher himself. Hyginus worked to defend the doctrine of the *Old Testament*. The *Liber Pontificalis*, credits him with regulating the clergy, by defining the various roles and duties as well as the ecclesiastical hierarchy within the Church. He also established that churches be dedicated. He died in 140, but not as a martyr as many believe; he is not listed as a Saint on the Universal Church Calendar, but he has remained so in several regional calendars. He was buried near Saint Peter's Basilica.

10 – **Saint PIUS I** (140-155). Born in the Friuli region in Aquileia, he was elected pontiff after four years without a Pope. Most sources credit him with establishing the day on which Easter is officially celebrated, defining it as the first Sunday after the full moon in March. He is attributed with the ordination of deacons, priests and bishops, as well as issuing a decree allowing baptism of heretics of the Judaic sects, if they converted. He is venerated as a martyr and even Dante wrote about his martyrhood in "*Paradiso*." After his death he was buried next to Saint Peter.

11 – **(Saint) ANICETUS** (155-166). Born in Syria, he met with many of the illustrious Christians of his day on their visits to Rome, including the Greek Bishop Polycarp with whom he discussed the official date for celebrating Easter. Given the two different customs, they decided to each follow the tradition of their Rite. Anicetus remained faithful to that of the Roman Rite established by Saint Peter and Polycarp to the Eastern Orthodox Rite, which celebrated Easter according the Jewish calendar. It is presumed that Anicetus did not die as a martyr. He was probably the first Bishop of Rome to be buried in the catacombs of San Calisto. Later, Pope Clement VIII moved his remains to Palazzo Altemps in Rome.

12 – **(San) SOTER** (166-175). Originally from Fondi in the region of Latium, he was elected Pope during the reign of Marcus Aurelius. He is remembered for his particular generosity regarding the Corinthian Church, which had been under grave persecution. For this reason, he was defined as the *"Charitable Pope."*
He was the first to establish the sacramental validity of marriage only if it had undergone the benediction of a priest. He prohibited women, who at the time were acquiring more involvement in sacred things, from touching the sacred utensils and from burning incense during liturgical ceremonies. He was buried in the Church of Saint Martino ai Monti in Rome.

13 – **Saint ELEUTHERIUS** (175-189). Of Albanian origin and a disciple of Anicetus, he sent two envoys, Fugazius and Damian, to England to convert the English to Christianity. He fought vehemently against the heretical currents that abounded in Rome at that time. Towards the middle of his pontificate, precisely in the year 180, the Roman Emperor Commodus issued a concession to the Christians. Eleutherius also abolished some formerly held notions on the pureness and impurity of foods that had been derived from Judaism. He was buried near the tomb of Saint Peter (Sacred Vatican Grottoes).

14 - **Saint VICTOR I** (189-199). Born in Africa, he lived during peaceful times under the reign of Emperor Commodus. He dedicated his time to extending the boundaries of Roman evangelisation.
He fought that Easter be celebrated according to the Roman Rite, on the Sunday after the full moon in March. To achieve this, he had to meet with the Bishops of the Eastern Rite, the opposition, who celebrated the holiday according to the calendar of the Jewish Rite.
During his pontificate, he changed the official liturgical language from Greek to Latin. He is also buried in the necropolis of Saint Peter's in the Vatican.

15 – **Saint ZEPHYRINUS** (199-217). During his pontificate there was a new insurgence of Christian persecutions by Septimius Severus. He found himself having to confront theological and doctrinal controversies during his reign, only some of which, he was able to resolve. He established the rule that on Easter, sacrament would be administered only to persons over 14 years of age. He defended the rite of baptism and the insolubility of matrimonial bonds. He is buried in Rome in the catacombs of Saint Callistus. Zephyrinus had a mild temperament and was indulgent with Christians, who had fallen into the sins of adultery and fornication.

16 - **Saint CALLISTUS I** (217-222). He was born in Rome in a part of the city referred to as Ravennatio, which is now known as Trastevere. He is credited with expanding the Christian community's most ancient cemetery complex, the catacombs located on Via Appia in Rome, which now carry his name. A large number of Christians were buried there, including 46 popes and over 170,000 martyrs.

He is also responsible for one of the most ancient Roman Basilicas, Saint Mary in Trastevere, which was constructed in the same place where a ferocious group of idolaters threw him from a window into a well. He died a martyr.

17 – **Saint URBAN I** (222-230). Born in Rome, he converted Saint Cecilia and her pagan husband Valerian to Christianity.

The two were condemned to death and on the same place they were martyred, Urban had the Church of Saint Cecilia built.

He began the acquisition of real estate by the Church.

It is uncertain if he is buried in the catacombs of Saint Callisto or not. Part of his relics were donated by Pope Nicholas I to the French King, Charles the Bald, in 862. The relics ended up in Auxerre, where Urban is celebrated as the patron saint of vineyard keepers.

18 – **Saint PONTIAN** (230-236). Roman by birth, he was elected Pope on July 21, 230 at a relatively peaceful time. Emperor Alexander Severus tolerated religious groups and had a positive attitude towards Christianity. He was even interested in Christian doctrine, but the situation changed with the rise of the new Emperor Maximus Thrax. Pontain was deported and condemned to forced labour in the Sardinian mines, after having abdicated the papal throne to Anterus in 235. He ordered the singing of Psalms and the reciting of "*Confiteor Deo*," before a death. Pontain died of hardship and suffering in 235. He is buried in the papal crypt in the Saint Callistus cemetery.

19 – **Saint ANTERUS** (235-236). Of Greek origin, he died only forty-three days after his pontificate began. Like his predecessor, he was martyred by Emperor Maximus Thrax.

During his pontificate, he began the official collection of acts and relics of the martyrs, ordering that they be gathered together and kept inside churches in a place called the *Scrinium*. This can be considered the first nucleus of the official Vatican Library.

The collection of acts was later burned by Emperor Diocletian. Anterus is buried in the papal crypt at the cemetery of Saint Callistus. In the crypt an engraved inscription was discovered in 1854 reading, "*Anteros Ep*i."

20 – **Saint FABIAN** (236-250). The historian Eusebius wrote that when the Christians gathered with the clergy to elect the new pontiff, Fabiano was returning from the countryside and a dove landed on his head. The assembled faithful, touched by the episode, elected him as Pope. Fabiano guided the Church under the peaceful reign of Emperor Philip the Arab, which allowed him to dedicate himself to organising the Roman diocese. He divided the city into seven administrative districts; each one was overseen by a deacon and aimed at charity and assistance. With the new Emperor Decius, he also fell under persecution and was condemned to death on January 20, 250. His body rests in the papal crypt of the Saint Callistus cemetery.

21 – **Saint CORNELIUS** (251-253). Due to persecution by Emperor Decius, the papal throne remained empty for a brief time before Cornelius was elected Pope in 251.

During his pontificate, Cornelius opposed the priest Novation, who had declared himself Pope. The priest was later excommunicated by a synod of bishops held in Rome by Cornelius. With the arrival of the new Emperor, Trebonius Gallus, the Pope was exiled to Civitavecchia where he died in June of 253, though he was probably not martyred.

He was buried by a Roman matron named Lucina in a crypt on her estate near the cemetery of Saint Callistus.

22 – **(Saint) LUCIUS I** (253-254). According to the *Liber Pontificalis,* he was born in Lucca, but in other more widely accredited editions he is listed as Roman. He was elected pontiff in June of 251. Immediately exiled to Civitavecchia, under the reign of Emperor Gallus, he returned to Rome under the reign of Valerian.

He was strongly against the cohabitation of non blood-related men and women, as well as deaconesses and clergymen. He died in the year 245, but there is no proof of him being martyred. Lucius is buried in the papal crypt at the catacombs of Saint Callistus. He is commemorated on March 4th each year. His pontificate lasted exactly eight months and ten days.

23 – **Saint STEPHEN I** (254-257). A Roman nobleman, titular priests and deacons with ecclesiastical standing elected him in the cemetery of Saint Callistus in front of the Christian community. He sustained that the validity of Euchese baptism conferred to the heretics, in contrast to the beliefs of Saint Cyprian the Bishop of Carthage. Stephen was exiled by Emperor Valerian.

It is said that soldiers decapitated him on the pontifical throne while he was officiating at a religious function in the catacombs of Saint Callistus. He is buried in Rome in the Church of San Silvestro in Capite.

24 – **Saint SIXTUS II** (257-258). Born in Athens, he was quite a studious man and a philosopher. His pontificate spanned a difficult period as he tried to restore peaceful relations between the Church of Rome and Carthage, over whether or not to rebaptise the heretics. He adopted a tolerant behaviour towards Dionysius, Bishop of Alexandria, who preferred re-baptism of the converted heretics.

Persecuted by Emperor Valerian, he was decapitated on the same episcopal throne of the cemetery of Pretestato near his tomb in the Catacombs of Saint Callistus.

25 – **Saint DIONYSIUS** (259-268). He was born in the Magna Grecia colonies, probably near Turio. The pontifical throne was entrusted to Dionysius after a year with no pontiff, due to Emperor Valerian's persecutions. Dionysius reordered the Roman parochial districts and is distinguished for his extensive activity in the field of defining dogma and for combating the heresy of his time.

On the death of Emperor Valerian in 260, his son Gallienus took the throne and was much more lenient with the Christians, allowing the new Pope to calmly dedicate himself to problems within the Church. He is buried in the cemetery of Saint Callistus.

26 – **Saint FELIX I** (269-274). Roman by birth, his pontificate was under the reign of Emperor Aurelian, who limited the freedom of the Christian cult, ordering their persecution. Felix began the tradition of burying the martyrs under altars and of celebrating mass on their sepulchres. He wrote a letter to the clergy in Alexandria in which he sanctioned the christological doctrine, admitting that the divinity and humanity of Jesus Christ are two distinct parts of the same person. Buried in the necropolis of Saint Callistus, he was transferred to the Church of Santa Prassede.

27 – **Saint EUTYCHIAN** (275-283). There is very little known about his pontificate. He was elected in January of the year 275 and is remembered for his piety. He buried hundreds of martyrs and suffered their same fate under the persecution of Emperor Numerian in 283.
He decided that the martyrs should be wrapped in a white sheet and dressed with the "*dalmatica,*" of Roman Emperors. He was buried in the papal crypt at the cemetery of Saint Callistus, then in 1659 his relics were taken to the gothic cathedral in the city of Sarzana, where an imposing marble statue was erected in his honour.

28 - **(Saint) CAIUS or GAIUS** (283-296). Born in Dalmatia and a nephew of Emperor Diocletian, he was probably martyred by decapitation. His execution however was not ordered by his uncle, but by Emperor Maximillian.
He is attributed with the decree stating that no one may access the episcopate without having already received the level of ositary, reader, acolyte, exorcist, subdeacon, deacon, and priest. Considering that according to other sources these regulations date back further, we should retain that Caius better defined them. His relics are kept in the private Barberini chapel in Rome.

29 – **Saint MARCELLINUS** (296-304). There are many conflicting stories and legends regarding this pontificate. He was elected Pope in 296 and governed the Church during the days of the terrible and ferocious persecutions by Emperor Diocletian. When an Imperial edict was passed to confiscate Christian wealth, Marcellinus followed the mandate without opposition. The assembly of bishops absolved him of responsibility but did not accept his penitence, in that way abstaining from condemning him. He was arrested twice and died a martyr on October 25 of 304. His sepulchre, in the Priscilla cemetery, was highly venerated for several centuries.

30 – **Saint MARCELLUS I** (308-309). After four years without a Pope, Marcellus I was elected as the new pontiff. He restored order to the Church in Rome under the reign of the new Emperor Maxentius after the persecutions by Diocletian.
He was quite severe with the *lapsi* (those who negated their faith during the persecutions). The required penalties provoked a great tumult among the people, so much so that the Emperor decided to expel the lapsed from Rome. He died in exile on January 16, 309. His remains were taken to Rome and buried in the cemetery of Priscilla.

31 – **Saint EUSEBIUS** (309). He was of Greek origin, probably born in the southern Italian Greek colonies of Magna Grecia. His pontificate was very brief, lasting from April 18th to August 17th of the year 309. Like his predecessor, Eusebius had to confront the difficult problems of the lapsed faithful and their penitence. This situation put him in a contrasting position with the antipope Heraclius, who backed the apostates who wanted to return to the Christian community. To bring peace, Emperor Maxentius exiled them both to Sicily where Eusebius died on August 17, 309 after a four month pontificate. He was buried in Saint Callistus and afterwards his body was taken to the Church of Saint Sebastien.

32 – **(Saint) MILTIADES** (311-314). Born in Africa, his pontificate took place during a time of great change for Christians. Constantine beat Emperor Maxentius in the Battle of Ponte Milvio (312). With the Milan edict, Christians obtained religious freedom within the Empire, which resulted in Christianity winning over paganism.
The goods confiscated during the reign of Emperor Diocletian were restored to the Church. Miltiades is responsible for the first building of the Basilica of Saint John in Lateran. He died January 11, 314. His body rests in the Church of Saint Sylvester in Capite.

33 – **Saint SYLVESTER I** (314-335). Born in Rome, one would expect important events to have taken place during his reign, due to the length of his pontificate. In reality it was one of the blandest of the century. Pope Sylvester I headed the Church during the reign of Constantine I, the first Christian emperor. With the potent political power and support of the Emperor, he defiladed many of his duties. He did not participate in the ecumenical council in Arles and Nicaea, called by Constantine to condemn the Arian heresy and establish religious peace in the African and Eastern provinces. Legends of every kind grew around Sylvester who, died in Rome on December 31, 335. His relics are kept in the Church of Saint Sylvester in Capite.

34 – **Saint MARK** (336). Roman born, Mark was pontiff from January 18th until October 7th of the year 336. His pontificate centred around the Arian heresy.
He is attributed with the decision that the Bishop of Ostia consecrates the Pope as well as the creation of the first calendar listing all of the religious holidays. He introduced the "*pallio*" (white woolen stole) which is still in use today, woven with blessed white lamb's wool and adorned with black crosses.
He is responsible for the building of the Basilica that carries his name in Rome. He was brought to his present resting place from the cemetery of Saint Balbina by Pope Gregory IV.

35 – **Saint JULIUS I** (337-352). He became Pope during the battle with the Arians, which the Nicaean council had not yet suppressed, working towards their decisive defeat. He defended and recredited Saint Anthanasius, who was condemned during the synod of Tyre by the Arians and the Eusebians in 335. He is responsible for building many of the churches in Rome, such as Santi Apostoli and Saint Mary in Trastevere. He died on April 12, 352 and was buried on Via Aurelia in the tomb of Saint Callipodio where he had built a Church. Hadrian I moved his remains, in 790, to the Church of Saint Mary in Trastevere where they are still kept.

36 – **LIBERIUS** (352-366). He was born in Rome to the Savelli family. Emperor Constant, protector of the Arians, ordered Pope Liberius to approve the condemnation of Anthanasius. He did not agree and was exiled for his refusal. During his absence, Archdeacon Felix II (considered by some as Pope and by others as antipope), governed the Church. He ordered that on fast days, one could not ask for credit payments or discuss arguments. In 338, Liberius returned to Rome and is responsible for the Basilica of Saint Mary Major on the Esquiline Hill. He died September 24, 366 and was buried in the Vatican Grottoes.

37 – **Saint DAMASUS I** (366-384). Born to a Spanish noble family, his was elected Pope on October 1, 366 against antipope Ursicinus, after three days of battle between the two opposing factions and countless dead and wounded. He was backed by Emperor Valentinian I and confirmed the supremacy of the Church in Rome over all of the others, designating the Roman Bishop as custodian of Orthodoxy in the West. His actions were not very efficient in resolving the internal controversies of the Eastern Church. He was the first Pope in history to be a patron of the arts. A literate man himself, he had the Sacred Scriptures translated from Hebrew and composed various metered verses for the tombs of the martyrs in the Roman catacombs. He is buried in Rome in the Church of San Lorenzo in Damaso.

38 – **Saint SIRICIUS** (384-399). Roman born, he was elected as pontiff after a strong opposition by the lords of Urbino.
After the reign of Saint Peter, he was the first to use the title "Pope".
An energetic man, like his predecessor, he fought to affirm the importance of the Bishop of Rome and the Apostolate in the West.
Under his pontificate the Basilicas of Saint Clement, Santa Pudenziana, and Saint Paul's Outside the Walls, were all restructured. He was buried in the cemetery of Priscilla, until Paschal II moved his relics to the Church of Santa Prassede.

39 – **Saint ANASTASIUS I** (399-401). Born in Rome to the Massimi family, he defended Orthodoxy against the doctrines of Donatus and Majorinus, considering their works heretical (except for the Latin version *"Of Princes,"* by Rufino.)
He fought against the followers of a sect practicing heterodox rites and ordered that priests stand up with their heads bowed during the reading of the New Testament. As a Pope, however, his reign was rather insignificant. He died December 19, 401. He is buried in Rome, on Via Ostiense above the catacombs of San Ponziano. He pontificate lasted little more than two years.

40 – **Saint INNOCENT I** (401-417). A believer in the Bishop of Rome's supreme authority over the Church, he tried to create liturgical uniformity, basing the standard on the Roman Rite. He sided with Giovanni Crisostomo who was hated by the Empress Eudoxia; she deposed him as the Patriarch of Constantinople. To combat the heresy of Pelagians, he condemned the Thesis of Pelagius, winning the approval and support of the Emperor and of the African Church. He died March 12, 417. According to James, he was the son of Anastasius I. His body was buried in the Roman Church San Martino ai Monti.

41 – **Saint ZOSIMAS** (417-418). A Greek priest, he was elected Pope on March 18, 417, nominated by his predecessor Innocent I.

His short-lived pontificate was difficult and troubled. He did all that was possible in the battle against the Pelagian heretics, Celsius and their followers, even condemning them in a letter known as "*Tractoria*" addressed to all of the churches.

Quite a moralist, he ruled that illegitimate children and servants could not be ordained as priests. He died December 26, 418. His body is conserved in the Basilica of San Lorenzo Outside the Walls. His pontificate lasted a year and a half.

42 – **Saint BONIFACE I** (418-422). Born in Rome, he was elected nearly simultaneously with antipope Eulalius, without much ado until Emperor Honorius Flavius officially recognized him. He was an able organizer and intervened against the Pelagians, by having Honorius condemn them. He vehemently defended the rights of the Church in the East, in particular the predominance of the Roman pontificate over all of the Eastern patriarchs, including the one in Constantinople. The city, having become the new capital of the empire, was referred to as the "*new Rome*" Boniface died September 4, 422 and was buried in the Vatican Grottoes.

43 – **Saint CELESTINE I** (422-432). Deacon of the Campania region, he was a friend of Saint Augustine, which aided him in resolving differences with the Church in Africa. He followed the ecclesiastical policies of Boniface I and fought against the Pelagians, especially in Great Britain and southern France. At the council of Ephesus in 431, he condemned Nestorius, who professed a heretical doctrine over the dual nature of Christ – the divine and the human – which he held as two fully distinct natures, not united but co-existing "accidentally" in moral union. He died July 27, 432 and was buried in Rome in the Church of Santa Prassede.

44 – **(Saint) SIXTUS III** (432-440). A Roman priest, he was a man of great diplomatic skill. He worked towards reconciling the doctrinal controversies that arose over the Nestorian Theory after the council of Ephesus.

He did much towards the reconstruction and embellishment of the Roman Basilicas that were destroyed during the "Sacking of Rome" by Alaricus, especially Saint Mary Major and Saint Paul's. In 440, he began the construction of San Lorenzo in Lucina. During his pontificate, Rome became more beautiful and sumptuous. He died August 19, 440 and is buried in San Lorenzo Outside the Walls.

45 – **Saint LEO I (the Great)** (440-461). Originally, from Volterra in the Tuscia region, he climbed the ecclesiastical ladder rapidly and was elected Pope unanimously by the clergy and the people. He quickly demonstrated his able capacity for governing by confronting Attila and forcing him to withdraw. He was not however, able to evade the Sacking of Rome in 455 by Genseric's Vandals. More so than his predecessors, he reinforced the supremacy of the Rome Bishop over all of the others. There are 96 of the sermons he wrote still in existence, which serve as a precious testimony to the ecclesiastical life of his times. He died November 10, 461 and his body lies in Saint Peter's Basilica under the altar dedicated to him.

46 – **Saint HILARIUS** (461-468). Born in Cagliari, the deacon Ilarius was the successor of Leo the Great. He participated in the council of Ephesus as the Roman legate and followed in the footsteps of Leo I in ecclesiastical and political matters. After his election as Pope, on November 19, 461, he dedicated himself to ordaining Churches beyond the Alps. He built and restored several sacred buildings, such as the oratory of the Lateran Baptistery, which is still in good condition today. He enriched the sacristies and treasuries of many Roman basilicas with gold and silver utensils, including the Basilica of Saint Peter 's and of Saint Paul's. He died February 29, 468 and his body lays in San Lorenzo Outside the Walls.

47 – **Saint SIMPLICIUS** (468-483). Born near Rome in Tivoli on March 3, 468. He was elected Pope during a period of incessant barbaric invasions that destroyed everything except the Vatican. During his pontificate, Romulus Augustulus became the Emperor in 476, marking the fall of the Roman Empire in the West. The schism that followed brought about the founding of new churches in Constantinople. Nevertheless, for the same reason, he gained more influence in the West. Simplicius reorganized the Church patrimony and regulated the distribution of charity to the poor. He sent priests far and wide, to help combat the Arian heresy. He died March 10, 483 and is buried in Saint Peter's Basilica.

48 - **Saint FELIX III** (483-492). Born in Rome, he took the name Felix III due to the presence of an antipope or due to an error in registration. He saw the rise of the conflicts with the Patriarch of Constantinople, Acacius. The Patriarch ignored the decisions of the council of Calcedonia (Christ is one person with a dual nature), and wanted to reinstate certain heretical movements approving the Henoticon edict, which favoured the Monophysites, who sustained that only one nature exists in Jesus Christ, human and divine at the same time. Felix III excommunicated him and deposed him. This gave rise to the Schism of Acacius, which lasted from 484 until 519. Felix died March 1, 492 and is the only Pope in history to be buried in the Basilica of Saint Paul's Outside the Walls.

49 – **Saint GELASIUS I** (492-496). Of African origin, he was an advisor to Felix III. He rose to the papal throne during the Schism of Acacia, avidly sustaining the Roman Church against the Eastern Empire of Anastasius.
He laid out the doctrinal foundations and defined policy regarding the temporal and spiritual power of the Pope in the Empire, which became the basis of the medieval period. Full of charity and benevolence for the poor, he began the construction of many basilicas surrounding Rome.
He died poor on November 21, 496 and is buried in Saint Peter's Basilica.

50 – **(Saint) ANASTASIUS II** (496-498). Born in Rome, he was consecrated Pope on November 24th. During his pontificate, he tried to find a compromise with Constantinople regarding the Schism of Acacius and even though he defended the Roman position, he was nearly considered a heretic for not taking a more aggressive stance.
At this time, Clodoveus, King of France, converted to Christianity and was baptized together with 3000 of his countrymen.
He died November 19, 498, and is buried in Saint Peter's Basilica. In Dante's "*Divine Comedy*," he was placed in "*Inferno*." He was Pope for nearly two years.

51 – **Saint SYMMACHUS** (498-514). Born in Sardinia, he was legitimized Pope by King Theodoric, when certain minor Byzantine factions nominated antipope Lorenzo. During the council of 499 at Saint Peter's, Symmachus established that a Pope could not nominate his successor. In the years that followed, his sustainers continued the struggle in the battle against Lorenzo until he finally withdrew and Symmachus was able to pass a few years in peace. He built the Church of San Pancrazio at Janiculum and San Martino ai Monti. He died July 19, 514, and was buried in Saint Peter's Basilica.

52 – **Saint HORMSIDAS** (514-523). A native of Frosinone, Ormsmida was elected one day after the death of Symmachus. After having reconciled the consequences of the schism caused by antipope Lorenzo, he was forced to face the even graver consequences of the schism of Acacius. The definitive reconciliation between the Church of the East and of the West happened during his pontificate. He demonstrated great authority and ability in the negotiations. Regarding ecclesiastical studies, he legislated that positions in the Church could not be given in exchange for privileges or donations. He died August 6, 523, and is buried in Saint Peter's Basilica.

53 – **Saint JOHN I** (523-526). Originally, from Tuscia (Tuscany), he was elected Pope August 13th and sent by King Theodore to the Emperor of the East, Justin II to obtain a cessation of the measures against Arianism. He was received with great honours; but on his return to Ravenna, Theodore threw him into prison. He was jailed for the partial failure of his ambassadorship; he only negotiated the parts that were in favour of the Church, without having all of the laws against the Arians revoked. He died in prison on May 18, 526. He was taken to Rome and was buried in the portico of Saint Peter's Basilica; the Church considers him a martyr.

54 – **Saint FELIX IV** (526-530). He was elected by the imperial nomination of Theodoric, to carry out his aims. However, Felix immediately demonstrated himself dedicated to the Church, and attracted the goodwill of the people. He gained great favour from the court of Ravenna, such as the power to judge the clergy in civil matters. Over fear of a schism, he passed the Papal robe to his successor Boniface II, but this unusual reaction actually provoked another schism in the Roman Church.
Felix died September 22, 530, and his body is buried in the Vatican Grottoes in Saint Peter's Basilica.

55 – **Saint BONIFACE II** (530-532). He became Pope at the request of his predecessor Felix IV. A schism was born when the clergy nominated archdeacon Dioscuro, but they lost fervour soon afterwards, when the competitor died.
Boniface dedicated himself to helping the poor in times of need, and he had the monastery built at Montecassino. The first publication of the biography of the popes, which was later called, *Liber Pontificalis*, dates back to these times.
Boniface died in Rome on October 17, 532 and is buried in the Vatican Grottoes at Saint Peter's Basilica.

56 – **JOHN II** (533-535). A Roman Pope with the given name Mercurius, but not being able to take the Papal throne with the name of a pagan divinity, he assumed the name John. He was the first of the popes to change his name once he was elected.

He fought against simony (the act of selling sacred objects or ecclesiastical titles) and formulated an important theory reaffirming the principle that only the human part of Christ had suffered martyrdom. With the Alarican edict, he established that he was head of all of the bishops. He died on May 8, 535, and his body is buried in the Vatican Grottoes at Saint Peter's.

57 – **Saint AGAPETUS I** (535-536). Born in Rome, to the Anicia family, he was elected Pope on May 13, 535: he condemned the tradition of the time allowing the Pope to choose his successor. He was sent by Theodatus, the Gothic King, to Constantinople to dissuade Emperor Justinian from setting his expansionistic sights on Italy. He was unsuccessful and died victim of the intrigues cause by the Emperor's wife, after having obtained the deposition of the monophystic Patriarch- Antimo.

He fell ill and died in Constantinople April 22, 536. He is buried in the Vatican Grottoes.

58 – **Saint SILVERIUS** (536-537). He was elected with the support of Gothic King Theodatus, who intended to use his influence against the court of Byzantium.

Son of Pope Ormsida, his pontificate was during the time in which Justinian's Byzantine troops, guided by Commander Belisarius, kicked the Goths out of Italy. Silverius was accused of plotting with the Goths who attacked Rome, so he was exiled to the island of Pona where he died on November 11, 537. He was buried on the same island. In his place the implacable Vigilius, who was backed by the Emperor's wife Theodora, became Pope.

59 – **VIGILIUS** (537-555). Born to a Roman noble family, he won the papal throne thanks to Empress Theodora of Byzantium, after the death of Silverius. After the conquest of the new King of the Goths, Vitiges, by Belisarius who defended the city of Rome in the name of Emperor Justinian, Vigilius found himself having to face all of the dangers associated with a long siege of troops. After two years of new attacks by Tilus, commander of the Goths, Vigilius was held as a prisoner of the Emperor for eight years, on orders from Justinian. He died in Syracuse during his return trip June 7, 555. He is buried in the Vatican Grottoes.

60 - **PELAGIUS I** (556-561). He substituted Vigilius with success during his forced absence from Rome. One year after the death of his predecessor, he was elected with the support of Justinian. To curry favour with the Emperor, he revoked previous decisions, underwriting the condemnation of Eutiche, and accepting the thesis of the council of Constantinople (6/2/553), favourable to the Nestorian heresy. These changes cost him the approval of the Romans and the support of his works on behalf of the military Byzantine government of Nareste.

Pelagius died March 4, 561 and his body is buried in Saint Peter's Basilica.

61 – **JOHN III** (561-574). Elected during the Longobard invasion, he had to wait for imperial recognition before being crowned. The sacking invaders were ruthless, in particular towards the bishops and the clergy.

He brought to bay the difficulties between the Churches of Ravenna and Milan, which were still diffident over the change of policy of Pelagius I, but he was unable to close the schism called *"Tre Capitoli"* from the name of the treatise with which Justinian condemned three writers inclined towards the Nestorian heresy. He finished the Roman Church of Santissimi Apostoli. He is buried in the Vatican Grottoes.

62 – **BENEDICT I** (575-579). Born in Rome, he was elected nearly a year after the death of his predecessor John III, with the Longobards camped outside the gates of Rome, interrupting all communication with Constantinople.

During his pontificate, Benedict fought to bring order back to the city of Rome, which was filled with plague and poverty due to the barbaric invasions. He confirmed the fifth council of Constantinople. Little else is known about the life of this Pope. At his death, which took place July, 30, 579, Benedict was buried in the sacristy of Saint Peter's Basilica.

63 – **PELAGIUS II** (579-590). Roman born of Gothic origins, he was consecrated without imperial approval during the siege of the Longobards in Rome. The Emperor of the East, Tiberius, was not able to give much help in liberating Rome. Pelagius asked the French King and received a temporary truce with Autari the Longobard.

Not long before his death, he witnessed the destruction of Montecassino monastery and the advancement of the plague and poverty that brought about his death as well on February 7, 590. His body is buried in Saint Peter's Basilica.

64 – **Saint GREGORY I THE GREAT** (590-604). Descendant of a Roman noble family, Anici, he participated in governmental life as a young man serving as prefect of Rome. Elected Pope, without the help of Byzantium, he negotiated with Agilulfo at the gates of Rome and persuaded him to spare the city. He protected the Jewish people from the excesses of the fanatics and encouraged Queen Teodolinda in the conversion of the Longobards. Gregory undertook a vast liturgical reform, giving the definitive compilation of the Roman missal and regulating the sacred Cantus. He died on March 12, 604 and is buried in the Clementine Chapel in Saint Peter's Basilica.

65 – **SABINIAN** (604-606). Born in Blera, in Tuscia (the ancient Etruria and present day Tuscany), he was elected Pope on September 13, 604. After the esteemed works of his predecessor, Sabinian was not able to win as much popular support as Gregory. The jealousy and envy that he himself felt for his predecessor, so admired and loved by the people, led him to only see hate and aversion around him. He was also accused of being miserly to the people stricken by poverty. He is counted as a transitional Pope. He died, possibly a violent death, on February 22, 606. He is buried without honours in Saint Peter's Basilica.

66 – **BONIFACE III** (607-607). Born in Rome of Greek origins, he was elected one year after the death of Sabinian. A short-lived pontificate, but of great importance because he managed to get Emperor Foca to promulgate an edict that recognized the only universal Bishop, meaning Pope, as the one in Rome. In the past, the title had also been used for the Bishop of Constantinople. He prohibited choosing a new Pope earlier than three days after the death of his predecessor. He died on November 12, 607 and is buried in the Vatican Grottoes.

67 – **BONIFACE IV** (608-615). A Benedictine monk, born in the region of Marsi, he was elected Pope ten months after the death of his predecessor Boniface III.
During his pontificate, he obtained the consensus of Emperor Foca, to transform the Pantheon from a pagan temple into a Christian Church, consecrating it to the cult of the Virgin "*Saint Mary of the Martyrs*" and had many of the martyrs' bodies carried there from the catacombs. He instituted the holiday of All Saints Day, which is celebrated on November 1st of every year.
Boniface died May 8, 615 and his body rests in the left transept of Saint Peter's Basilica.

68 – **Saint ADEODATUS I or DEUSDEDIT** (615-618). Born in Rome, he was elected Pope five months after the death of Boniface IV. In this period, the aversion towards Byzantium's authority provoked a rebellion in Ravenna, Naples and Rome. Adeodatus is remembered for the good relations that he was able to keep with Byzantium, notwithstanding the rebellions, as well as for the charity he showered upon victims of a terrible earthquake and plague which violently struck the people in 615. He was the first to use the pontifical seal to close papal bulls and decrees. He died November 8, 615 and is buried in the Vatican Grottoes.

69 – **BONIFACE V** (619-625). He was of Neapolitan origin and rose to the throne of Saint Peter's on December 23, 619, merely one year later he gained imperial confirmation. He is remembered for the ratification of the"*right to asylum*," which provided that no one could be hunted if they had found refuge inside a Church, a sacred place or a monastery. This right of immunity, emanated by his predecessors, was generally ignored. In 622, during the years of his pontificate, a fact of considerable importance happened: *Hegira*, when Mohammed moved from Mecca to Medina, an event that signified the beginning of the Muslim era. He did much to spread Christianity throughout England. He is buried in the Vatican Grottoes.

70 – **HONORIUS I** (625-638). He was from a noble family of the Campania Region and was elected by the people and the clergy with great expectations. A capable administrator of the Church's patrimony, he spent large sums on restoring and building numerous Roman churches. In the area of doctrine and dogma, however, he did not have the same success and was even accused of sharing the heretical ideas of the monothelists from the letters he wrote to Sergius, the heretical Patriarch of Constantinople. Many years later, in 680, at the third council of Constantinople, he was condemned. In the words of Leo II, "He did not make every effort to defend the Catholic Church." He died October 12, 638 and he is buried in the Vatican Grottoes.

71 – **SEVERINUS** (640). His election, in 638, was confirmed and recognized twenty months later by Emperor Eraclius who tried in vain during that time to obtain approval of the edict Echtesis, which legitimized monothelism (a heretical theory). Severinus naturally refused to sign it, even after the promise that his messengers made in Constantinople in exchange for the *placet*. The anger of Eraclius was unleashed and he sent his ministers to take a good part of the Lateran treasure accumulated by Honorius. Severinus died August 2, 640 after only two months as Pope. He is buried in the Vatican Grottoes.

72 – **JOHN IV** (640-642). Of Dalmatian origin, he was consecrated Pope December 24, 640 only four months after the death of his predecessor. Like the Pope before him, he condemned monothelism and thus the Patriarch of Constantinople. He made an apology defending the works of Pope Severinus, who had been accused of having too little conviction in regards to the heresy. He helped his fatherland and his co-nationals who were oppressed by the Slavs, by sending large sums to ransom the slaves. He had the bodies of three martyrs; Venanzio, Anastasius, and Mauro sent to Rome and dedicated a chapel in the Vatican to them. He died October 12, 642.

73 – **THEODORE I** (642-649). Of Greek origin, he was elected only one month after the death of John IV. He was also firmly set against the heretical monothelist movement that was strengthened at the time by the edict *Tipus*, with which Emperor Constance II prohibited all debate over controversial theological definitions, in particular those regardingthe double or singular will of Christ. Everybody was forced to keep their opinions to themselves and even the Pope could not speak of it. The edict, naturally did not resolve the dispute, but did manage to provoke great resentment. Theodore died May 14, 649 and is buried in Saint Peter's Basilica.

74 – **Saint MARTIN I** (649-655). Originally from Todi in Umbria, he was consecrated Pope in July of 649, but did not have the consensus of Emperor Constance II. With great energy and resolution, he fought against the monothelist heresy for the reaffirmation of orthodoxy. In a council held at Lateran on October 5, 649, he strongly condemned two works. *Ecstesis* by Eraclius and *Tipus* by Constance II. To vindicate himself, Emperor Constance II sent the exarch Olympus to Rome, to arrest Martin. The mission failed, but the second time around, Martin was taken prisoner. After much humiliation and suffering, he was exiled to Chersonese and deposed. He is buried in the Church of San Martino ai Monti.

75 – **Saint EUGENE I** (654-657). Roman born son of Rufino, he was consecrated Pope by Emperor Constance II when Pope Martin I was on his way to prison in Constantinople. The papal seat therefore, was not vacant, but the acceptance of the pontificate on behalf of Eugene, was made out of fear that Constance II would choose a monothelist Pope. He was able to change his image only with his refusal to accept an ambiguous profession of faith (the Synodical), sent to him by the Patriarch Peter, somewhat raising the level of his pontificate, which was weak and seconded the temporal power of the times. He is buried in the Vatican Grottoes.

76 – **Saint VITALIAN** (657-672). To re-establish peace with Emperor Constance II, Vitalian, elected July 30, 657, kept very diplomatic relations with Constantinople and received the Emperor with a solemn and unwarranted welcome when he came to Rome on an official visit July 5, 663. The Emperor played the part and demonstrated himself devoted and friendly, but in reality, it was only a superficial and obsequious action. Before leaving, he ordered the cruel sacking of Rome. In this time, the Longobards definitively converted to Christianity. Vitalian died January 27, 672 and his body lies in the Vatican Grottoes.

77 – **ADEODATUS II** (672-676). Roman born and a Benedictine monk in the monastery of Saint Erasmus al Celio, he was elected April 11, 672. He was much admired for the generosity and wealth of spirit that he treated everyone with, without distinction. He was not however of great religious or political importance.
A peaceful pontificate characterized by the weakening of the Byzantine presence in Italy and the beginnings of the conversion of the Maronites (population of Armenian-Syrian origin). He died June 17, 676 and his body rests in the Vatican Grottoes.

78 – **DONUS** (676-678). Born in Rome, he rose to the pontificate November 2, 676. During this time, the schism between Ravenna and Rome that had protracted throughout the reign of Vitalian, finally halted. Donus, with the help of Emperor Constantine IV Pogonat, with whom he had an optimal friendship of reciprocal collaboration, managed to convince Archbishop Theodore to accept the Pope's authority. The Emperor himself proposed to hold a conference between the bishops to resolve the divergences between the Church of the East and the West. During the preparations for the grand event, Donus died on April 11, 678. He is buried in the Vatican Grottoes.

79 – **Saint AGATHO** (678-681). Born in Palermo, he was elected Pope two months after the death of Donus. He worked to reconcile the dissidence between Byzantium and Rome. In 680, he called a synod to prepare for the sixth ecumenical council. It opened in Constantinople on November 7, 680 with the Emperor presiding. In front of an assembly formed of Eastern and Western delegations, he approved the doctrine of the dual nature and will of Christ, thereby condemning the heretical monothelists. The council also condemned Honorius I for having been too indulgent and ambiguous about resolving the heresy. He died at the age of 107! He is buried in Saint Peter's Basilica.

80 – **Saint LEO II** (682-683). Born in Catania, he was consecrated Pope on August 17, 682 after a long wait for imperial confirmation. The condemnation of Honorius at the ecumenical council in Constantinople required that the entire ecumenical world accept the sentence, and the Emperor waited to confirm Leo, until they had. Leo immediately approved all of the acts of the council and detailed the reasons for the condemnation of Pope Honorius, confirming it with a letter to the Emperor. An eloquent and cultured Pope, during his brief pontificate he managed to restore the Church of Saint George in Velabro and Saint Bibiana. He died July 3, 683 and his body is buried in Saint Peter's under the altar of the chapel of the Madonna of the Colonna.

81 – **Saint BENEDICT II** (684-685). Born in Rome to the wealthy Savelli family, he was consecrated Pope on June 26, 684. Once again, there was a long wait before imperial confirmation finally arrived. The pious Emperor, Constantine IV Pogonat, realizing the difficulties that it implied, wrote a letter stating that imperial confirmation was no longer required for papal elections. He wrote that instead, the exarch of Ravenna's confirmation would suffice, deciding it would be much simpler that way. Benedict was a patient and humble Pope and was highly esteemed by the Emperor. He died May 8, 685 and was buried in Saint Peter's, in the Vatican Grottoes.

82 – **JOHN V** (685-686). Born in Syria, he was elected July 23, 685, and was chosen by the Emperor. During this particular time in history, the pontificates were rather brief due to the advanced age of the pontiffs at the time of their elections. John V had served as legate to Pope Agatho at the sixth ecumenical council in Constantinople, though he was not able to actively participate due to a serious ailment. He did manage to regulate the nominations for Sardinian bishops, which before that time had been decided arbitrarily without approval by the Sainted Seat. He died August 2, 686 and was buried in Saint Peter's Basilica.

83 – **CONON** (686-687). Elected on October 21, 686, he was originally from Tracia. He was already very ill at the moment of his election, which was probably one of the reasons he was nominated. Two other hopeful candidates from two different factions were contending for the papal throne and his election bought them some time. The new Emperor Justinian II, the son of Constantine Pogonat, put great amounts of imperial pressure on the Roman Church, which did not bode well for the future. During his short and difficult reign, Conon made several auspicious donations. He died September 2, 687 and was buried in Saint Peter's Basilica.

84 - **Saint SERGIUS I** (687-701). Most likely of Syrian origin, his pontificate lasted 14 years and was rich with important events in the Church and in Italy. When Sergius was elected Pope, two antipopes had been elected: the archdeacon Paschal and the archpriest Theodore, but the discord did not last for long. Sergius I had a difficult bout with the new Emperor Justinian II, who held a council in Constantinople, in 691, without inviting the Pope or asking his approval. Sergius was later saved from being arrested, by the Byzantine insurrection in Ravenna and in Pentapoli (union of five towns). His arrest was ordered after he sternly protested to approve the measures of the aforesaid council. He is buried in the Vatican Grottoes.

85 – **JOHN VI** (701-705). Of Greek origin, he had strained relations with the Emperor of the East, Justinian II, who tried to influence papal decisions by using his immense temporal power to try and sway the pontiff's opinion on many contradictory arguments and controversies of the time. John was in strong opposition to the Emperor and had the support of the Italian people, who were tired of being prevaricated upon by Constantinople's policies and had started to take their distance. The Turks had begun to expand into Europe, posing grave dangers to the Christians. John is buried in the Vatican Grottoes.

86 – **JOHN VII** (705-707). This Pope, of Greek origin, was elected a very short time after his predecessor. He continued the peaceful policy of his predecessors and consolidated the temporal power of the popes by requiring the Longobard King Heribert II to give back certain territories of the Transylvanian Alps (Cozie). He effectively opposed Justinian's desire to win back Italy, in terms of power and respect.

John VII favoured the building of monasteries including those in Subiaco and Farfa as well as important works in the city of Rome. He is buried in the Vatican Grottoes.

87 – **SISINNIUS** (January 15-February 4, 708). Originally from Syria, he was already very ill when he was elected Pope, (so afflicted by gout that he had to be fed by hand). He died just twenty days after his election, making his pontificate one of the shortest in history.

He began the collection funds for the restoration of the Aurelian Walls in Rome, which had been practically destroyed after the many assaults on the city during the battles with the Longobards. He died of gout and was buried in the Vatican Grottoes.

88- **CONSTANTINE** (708-715). Born in Syria, in contrast with his predecessors, he had a good relationship with Emperor Justinian II, who confirmed the privileges conceded to the Church and pushed the Bishop of Ravenna, who was independent from Rome, to submit to the authority of the Pope. Philipicus Bardanes, who proclaimed himself Emperor, killed Justinian. Philipicus was a Monothelite. He had the acts of the sixth ecumenical council burned and assumed a hostile attitude towards the Pope. Soon, there was a rebellion against Philipicus, who was dethroned by Anastasius II. He is buried in the Vatican Grottoes.

89 – **Saint GREGORY II** (715-731). He affirmed the autonomy of the Roman Church in light of the Longobard expansionism and the iconoclast politics of the Eastern Emperor. In 726, when Leo III, the sovereign of Constantinople, prohibited the cult of sacred images, Paul the exarch of Ravenna supported him and started a rebellion. The Longobard King Liutprando, who hoped to use the occasion to his advantage to get his hands on Rome, supported five Italian cities, united in a group known as Pentapoli. Gregory II managed to convince Liutprando to desist attacking Rome and persuaded him to give up and to donate his castle in Sutri to Saint Peter's. He is buried in the Vatican Grottoes.

90 – **Saint GREGORY III** (731-741). Of Syrian origin, as soon as he was elected Pope, he called a council at Saint Peter's to condemn iconclasty and excommunicate its followers. In Italy, the war heated back up between the Pope and Liutprando the Longobard who had ignored his promise of submission to Gregory II. In 739, the Pope asked Charles Martel (the French King) to intervene and help stop Liutprando's repeated invasions of the Roman dukedom. Charles did not come to the Pope's defence, but the foundations for future popes looking to France to help defend the pontificate, had been laid. Gregory III is credited with the construction of an Oratory in the Vatican Basilica and for covering the Pantheon with sheets of lead. He is buried in the Vatican Grottoes.

91 – **Saint ZACHARY** (741-752). Born in Greece, he managed to reconcile with Liutprando and stipulated a twenty-year truce, as the political detachment between Rome and Byzantium took place. Not long before his death, Charles Martel, the French King, validated the donations made by Liutprando to the Church. On the death of King Charles, his son Pepin the Short was elected as regent for Childeric III of the Merovingians. He asked the Pope's help to become the rightful King and Pope Zachary bestowed a royal investiture on Pepin the Short, crowning him as King of France. This time it was the Pope to give the *placet* to the Emperor. He is buried in the Vatican.

92 – **STEPHEN II (III)** (752-757). Roman by birth, he was elected after a brief reign of another candidate with his same name, who was never consecrated. The Pope continued to cultivate bonds with the French, asking Pepin's help against Astolfo's (the Longobard King who succeeded Liutprando) bullying. Stephen II went to France in 754, to consecrate Pepin as King of France in the Church of Saint Denis, nominating him *"Patrician of the Romans,"* which further reinforced his prestige. When the Pope asked for his help in protecting the Church, Pepin came to the pontiff's aid. He won against Astolfo in Pavia and took the exarchate of Ravenna away from and gave it to the Pope. He is buried in the Vatican Grottoes.

93 – **Saint PAUL I** (757-767). Brother of Pope Stephen II and Roman by birth, he was elected Pope when his brother was too sick too rule, in opposition to archdeacon Theophylactus, who was backed by a different party. Paul I continued to build the friendship with Pepin. He still needed him to get back the lands that Desiderius, the Longobard King who succeeded Astolfo, had decided not to give back. Pepin did his best to mediate and negotiate with Desiderius as well as with Constantine V, the King of Byzantium. He was a good and charitable Pope and did much towards establishing friendly relations with the Greek Church. He is buried in the Vatican Grottoes.

94 – **STEPHEN III (IV)** (768-772). Born in Sicily, in the city of Syracuse, he was elected Pope in a period of great turmoil between rival factions that both wanted to elect their own representatives: one lay, Constantine II and his priest, Fillip, who returned to the monastery the day he was elected. Affronting a delicate subject, Stephen called a council in which it was established that one could not be elected Pope if he had not first been elected Cardinal. He did not have success opposing the marriages of Pepin's heirs. Charles and Carleman married the daughters of Desiderius The latter was much in favour of the union hoping it would give him a bit of relief from French influence in the Italian territories. He is buried in the Vatican Grottoes.

95 – **ADRIAN I** (772-795). Born to the royal Roman family Colonna, he broke away from King Desiderius and pushed to end the Longobard reign in Italy. He turned to the French King Charlemagne, against Desiderius. The Pontifical State, referred to as *"Patrimony of Saint Peter,"* was very vast at this time. Adrian I nominated Charlemagne as *"Patrician of Rome,"* who, with the title accepted the responsibility of protecting the Italian territory. He assured jobs and economic stability to the inhabitants of his territories and he worked on many renovation and building projects including putting new façades on many churches and laying the foundations for Santo Spirito Hospital. He is buried in the Vatican.

96 – **Saint LEO III** (795-816). This Roman Pope, elected two days after the death of his predecessor, was threatened and taken prisoner by Adrian I. Freed by the Roman people, he took refuge in France and asked Charlemagne's intervention before taking office in Saint Peter's. In recognition, Leo III crowned Charlemagne as Emperor on Christmas Eve of the year 800. With the privilege of crowning sovereigns, the Pope acquired religious authority above the Emperor's political authority, but the Emperor had the right to confirm pontifical elections. On Charlemagne's death, in 814, Rome was turned upside down with battles and plots. He was buried in Saint Peter's.

97 – **STEPHEN IV (V)** (816-817). Born to a noble family, he was unanimously elected by the people and then moved into Saint Peter's without waiting for authorization from the new French Emperor Ludwig the Pious, Charlemagne's son. A short time later, in the interest of maintaining good relations with the empire, Stephen IV went to Reims, where he crowned Ludwig as Emperor, together with his wife Ermengarde. The Emperor, in turn, confirmed the donations made to the Church by his father as well as promising to continue to protect the papacy. His pontificate was very short: he died in January of 817, only seven months after his election; he was buried in the Vatican.

98 – **Saint PASCHAL I** (817-824). A Roman monk, of the Massimo family, he was elected Pope the day after Stephen IV's death, to avoid any meddling by Ludwig the Pious. Soon afterwards, Paschal sent a legate to the Emperor asking him to confirm papal ownership of the lands donated to the Church, by Pepin and Charlemagne. During Easter of the year 823, he crowned Ludwig's son Lothair, as Emperor, recognizing his authority over Rome. Paschal is remembered for exhuming the Christian martyrs, from the catacombs as well as for missionary activities and the evangelization of Denmark and Scandinavia. He is buried in the Vatican Grottoes.

99 – **EUGENE II** (824-827). He was also Roman born, elected in a moment of turmoil, because Cardinal Zinzinio hoped to become Pope and opposed Eugene's nomination. Under his pontificate, Lothair went to Rome and issued a document known as the "*Consititutio Romana*," which regulated relations between the Pope, the Empire, and Rome. Eugene, in return instituted a commission to regulate the application of the laws. He was not an able Pope in political matters, so much so in fact, that he fell under domination of Aquisgrana. He called a council in which decisions were made regarding the faith. He is buried in the Vatican Grottoes.

100 - **VALENTINE** (August-September 827). Roman born, he was a deacon and was archdeacon under Paschal I.
When he was elected Pope, his election was not communicated to Emperor Lothair.
He was a very devoted and virtuous man, much loved by the Romans from the beginning. With such a short pontificate, lasting little over a month, he did not really have enough time to accomplish much in any area. However, during the time he reigned, he had coins minted (in the Vatican Collections, there is a 22 millimetre example from his pontificate). He is buried in the Vatican Grottoes.

101 – **GREGORY IV** (827-844). Born in Rome, to a noble family, he was Cardinal of Saint Mark's. He got into a controversy regarding the repartitioning of imperial territories between the imperial families of Ludwig the Pious and his children. He was also very worried about problems in his home city, having to affront frequent incursions by the Saracen pirates on the city. In the Ostia area, near the sea, he had a town and fortress built, calling it Gregoriopolis. He is also credited with the beautiful mosaics in Saint Mark's. He worked towards the evangelization of the Nordic countries. He is buried in the Vatican Grottoes.

102 – **SERGIUS II** (844-847). At the time of his election, he was in opposition with the deacon John, who was supported by the people. Once he was elected, his antagonist became antipope. Sergius II took the pontifical seat without asking for imperial confirmation. For this, Lothair I sent his son Ludwig to Rome, asking Sergius II for confirmation of the imperial authority bestowed upon him in the *Constitutio Romana* of 824, stating that pontifical elections had to be approved by the Emperor. As a sign of consensus, Sergius elected Ludwig as King of Italy in 844. The terrible attack of the Saracens, who landed at Ostia, took place during his pontificate. The siege was terrible and they made many dramatic incursions into Rome. He is buried in the Vatican Grottoes.

103 – **Saint LEO IV** (847-855). Right after his election, Leo IV's first big responsibility, was affronting the question of the Saracens. Having settled in Ostia, they represented a grave threat. Leo had the walls surrounding Saint Peter's and Castel Sant'Angelo rebuilt, but the Saracens burned Borgo Leonine next to the castle. To neutralize the Saracen threat, the Pope allied the sea cities of Naples, Amalfi and Gaeta to obtain a decisive victory over the Saracens during the naval Battle of Ostia in 849. He is buried in the Colonna Chapel in Saint Peter's Basilica.

104 – **BENEDICT III** (855-858). Born in Rome, he was elected Pope against antipope Anastasius III, who was supported by Lothair and Ludwig.
After imperial troops tried to place Anastasius on the throne with the support of Bishop Arsenius, the Roman people resisted so fiercely, that Benedict was allowed to return to his post. Benedict III was much loved by the people for his generosity and sensitivity. He dedicated himself with care and dedication to many works of charity for the needy. He was Pope for little over two years. He is buried in Saint Peter's Basilica, in the Vatican Grottoes.

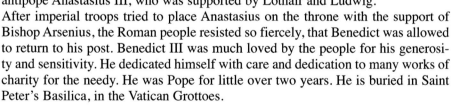

105 – **Saint NICHOLAS I** (858-867). He left a strong imprint on the history of the papacy, being one of the first popes to assume the role of absolute monarch. Many important changes took place during his pontificate and he made many decisions regarding the Church of Rome. He reinforced the temporal power of the Church and the primacy of the Pope over all of the churches. After years of antagonism with Fozio, the Patriarch of Constantinople, he saw the rise of the schism with the Church of the East that would last centuries. Nicholas made many important innovations regarding trial law, prohibiting torture and judicial proof. He fixed the commemoration of the Assumption of Mary on August 15th and was made a Saint, in 1600, by Urban VIII. He is buried in the Vatican Grottoes.

106 - **ADRIAN II** (867-872). Roman born and related to Pope Sergius II, he had been married as a young man and had two daughters. He was elected pontiff when he was in his eighties, after having already refused the pontifical crown twice. Even though he was advanced in age, he was very active. In 869, he called the fourth ecumenical council of Constantinople, in which Fozio's excommunication was confirmed. Adrian united the Roman Church with Moravia, welcoming the apostles Cyrillus and Methodius in Rome. The Pope nominated Methodius as Archbishop of Pannoni, with the duty of organizing the Christian community in those lands. He died exactly five years after his election. He is buried in the Vatican Grottoes.

107 – **JOHN VIII** (872-882). Roman, he was elected, contrary to the rules, Pope on the same day that his predecessor died. At the death of Ludwig II, the Pope using his leverage, preferred to crown Charles the Bald as Emperor in 875 and not Carleman. The fall of Carleman in Italy, the escape and death of Charles the Bald and the occupation of Rome pushed John VIII to flee to France. After returning to Italy, when the situation had abated, he allied against the Saracens with Carlo the Fat, the deceased Carleman's brother, crowning him Emperor in 881. But Charles did not maintain his promises and departed. The Pope settled with the Byzantines, obtaining victories in southern Italy. He is buried in the Vatican Grottoes.

108 – **MARINUS I** (882-884). Of English origins, he was born in a town in the region of Latium and was the first Bishop to ever become Pope. His first act of office was Fozio's re-excommunication for schismatic theories, after his papal predecessor John VIII had confirmed Fozio as Patriarch of Constantinople. He corrected another of his predecessor's errors when he reinstated Formosus, who had been unjustly accused by John VIII, as Bishop of Porto. Marinus I suffered terribly in 883 when Arab forces destroyed the monastery of Montecassino. He was only Pope for a year and a half and it is said that he died by poisoning. He is buried in the Vatican Grottoes.

109 – **Saint ADRIAN III** (884-885). Born in Rome, he was elected Pope in May of the year 884. He refused to give in to Emperor Basilius of the East, who pressured him for the annulment of Fozio's excommunication. Adrian established that, imperial confirmation was unnecessary to consecrate the Pope.
While he was on his way to France, invited by Emperor Charles the Fat to participate at the Diet of Worms, he died en route and was buried in the Abbey of Nonantolo, near Modena. He was proclaimed Saint, but the nomination was challenged until June of 1891 when he was finally sainted.

110 – **STEPHEN V (VI)** (885-891). During this pontificate, the problems with Fozio finally came to an end in 886, when the new Eastern Emperor, Leo VI, deposed Fozio, confining him to a monastery. The Holy Roman Empire became divided, due to the failing power of the Carolingian dynasty. Three states were born from its remains - France, Italy and Germany (which retained the imperial Crown). The Marquis of Friuli, Berenger, and Duke Guido of Spoleto sought to rule Italy. The latter was crowned in 891, by Pope Stephen, in exchange for recognizing the concessions and donations made by the French to the Church.

111 – **FORMOSUS** (891-869). He was born in Ostia (Roma). Elected Cardinal in 864, he was excommunicated by Pope John VIII, then later declared innocent by Marinus I, then finally became Pope in 891. The next year, he crowned Guido of Spoleto's son, Lambert, as Emperor. Later, due to prevarication by the two, he had to call on the King of Germany, Arnulf of Carinthia, to defend him. Not long later, Formosus died and the Spoleto faction decided to wreak revenge with a macabre farce. They exhumed his cadaver and carried out a mock trial, declaring him an unworthy and illegitimate Pope. Formoso's cadaver was then thrown into the Tiber, where a monk later recovered it. Afterwards, he was buried in Saint Peter's Basilica.

112 – **BONIFACE VI** (896). Born in Rome, he was elected Pope by Emperor Lambert of Spoleto's feudal sustainers against Arnulf of Carinthia's faction. The recent division of the empire had come about as a consequence of the growing power in the feudal states. At that time the pontifical seat was at the mercy of large fiefs in central Italy, in particular of Duke Guido of Spoleto, born of Roman nobility and the marquis of Tuscany. The pontificate of Boniface VI lasted merely fifteen days. He is buried in Saint Peter's in the Vatican Grottoes. Boniface VI had the shortest pontificate in history.

113 – **STEPHEN VI (VII)** (896-897). Roman, he was elected Pope by the sustainers of Duke Lambert of Spoleto, as was Boniface VI. After he was elected, to please the Duke of Spoleto, he dug up the cadaver of Formosus and held a macabre trial. The final judgement was a total condemnation of Formosus, guilty only of having preferred Arnulf of Carinthia to Duke Lambert of Spoleto. Stephen VI, hated by the people, had a cruel end to his life. In 897, during a public riot, he was arrested and put in prison, where a short time later he was strangled. He is buried in the Vatican Grottoes.

114 – **ROMANUS** (August-November 897). Born in Gallese in the Latium Region and brother of Pope Marinus I (882-884), he was elected Pope by the partisan sustainers of Formosus, with whom he had been friends. During the four short months of his pontificate, he worked to redeem the memory of Pope Formosus and he overturned the acts that his predecessor, Stephen VI, had drawn up against Formosus. He issued a papal bull giving the Spanish Church dominion over Majorca and Minorca. He died in November of 897, closed in a monastery, possibly due to poisoning and was buried in Saint Peter's Basilica.

115 –**THEODORE II** (897). He was born in Rome. Pope for merely twenty days, he was most likely assassinated in December of the year 897. The favoured candidate of the Germanic groups, he continued the work of redeeming the memory of Pope Formosus, deciding that he be buried in Saint Peter's. He overturned all of the decrees and rulings of the council known as "cadaverico," held by Stephen VI. He also called back and reinstated all of the bishops and clergymen that had been exiled. Theodore is also buried in Saint Peter's in the Vatican Grottoes.

116 – **JOHN IX** (898-900). Born in Tivoli, he was a Benedictine monk. Sustained by the Formosa faction, he was in contrast with Sergius III. He also worked towards redeeming the memory of Pope Formosus. He exiled and excommunicated the cardinals who had been accomplices of Stephen VI against Formosus, including Sergius who would become Pope in 904. On request from the Senate and the people of Rome, he sanctioned that the Roman episcopate and clergy elect the Pope. He confirmed Lambert of Spoleto as Emperor, but he died just a few months later. In regards to the Greek Church, he took a reconciliatory approach, recognizing the Patriarchs, Ignatius and Fozio, as legitimate. He is buried in the Vatican Grottoes.

117 – **BENEDICT IV** (900-903). Roman born, he was elected Pope during the first months of the year 900. He is remembered for having called the Lateran synod. He tried in vain to control the widespread corruption of the times.

In Rome during the year 901, he crowned Ludwig of Burgundy, King in Pavia, chosen by the Italian people, as Emperor. Benedict IV was a generous and well-intentioned man. He helped and accorded privileges to various monasteries. He was Pope for nearly three and a half years and is buried in the Vatican Grottoes.

118 – **LEO V** (July-September 903). From the Latium region, he was a Benedictine Cardinal. Even though he did not belong to the Roman clergy, he was elected Pope in 903. The chaplain Christopher, priest of San Damaso Church in Rome, imprisoned him and took advantage of his extremely weak character, to convince the Pope to abdicate, usurping his place in the meantime. Christopher was considered antipope until a few months later when he was taken prisoner and died violently in prison. Leo V retired to a monastery where he lived until his assassination, which might have been ordered by Sergius, who became the next Pope. Leo V is buried in the Vatican Grottoes.

119 – **SERGIUS III** (904-911). Born in Rome, he was one of the most questioned popes in the history of the Church. He was elected the first time in 898, backed by the Duke of Spoleto's faction, in opposition to Pope John IX. The latter excommunicated him and condemned him to exile. After a few years of exile, he was freed by Leo V and Christopher and returned to Rome. After gaining the support of Adalberto the Marquis of Tuscany, he was re-elected pontiff in 904. He had the Lateran Basilica rebuilt in 897 after it was destroyed by fire. He is remembered for his prevarications and sentimental relationships. He is buried in the Vatican Grottoes.

120 – **ANASTASIUS III** (911-913). This Roman Pope was elected right after Sergius on the basis of his impeccable morality and his virtuous behaviour, a quality which had been lacking in his predecessor.

Unfortunately, his honesty did not save him from his weakness, allowing Berenger I, the Bishop of Pavia to take advantage of numerous privileges and have many concessions. During his pontificate, a large number of Normans located in a northern region of France, converted to Christianity. The name Normandy derives from them. He died by poisoning and is buried in Saint Peter's Basilica in the Vatican Grottoes.

121 – **LANDO** (913-914). Originally from the Sabine region, he was Pope for only a few months, from July 913 until February of 914. In reality, there is very little known about his short pontificate. There are no records regarding the life he led before becoming Pope, nor of exactly how many months his pontificate actually lasted.

We can assume that, he probably followed the corrupt aristocratic-cleric behaviour of the period to manage his papal power. He no longer had any need to depend on imperial protection, since he was quite able to defend himself. It is assumed that he died a violent death. He is buried in Saint Peter's Basilica, in the Vatican Grottoes.

122 – **JOHN X** (914-928). Born in the Imola province in 860, he was elected Pope in 914, sustained by Theophylact and his wife Theodora. He was very active in religious matters. He is responsible for resolving the schism between the Eastern and the Roman Church. In political matters, he crowned Berenger as Emperor in 915. With his help he was able to form an alliance to combat the Saracens, who had settled on the borders of the pontifical lands. Once cleared out of those territories, the Saracens were defeated in June 916. After a grave run in with Marozia and her husband Guido of Tuscany, he was taken prisoner and declared as deposed. He was killed, most likely due to suffocation in 928. He is buried in Saint John in Lateran.

123 – **LEO VI** (May-December 928). The pontiffs following John X were backed by Marozia, the daughter of Theodora. She dominated the temporal power of Rome and was referred to as "*senatrix e patricia.*"

Born in Rome, Leo VI was an honest man, who during worked to end the discord that plagued Rome during his pontificate. He fought victoriously against the Saracens and the ferocious Hungarians. He wrote an encyclical to the bishops of Dalmatia, encouraging their obedience to their leader, John, the Archbishop of Spoleto. He died in December of 928 and is buried in Saint Peter's, in the Vatican Grottoes.

124 - **STEPHEN VII (VIII)** (928-931). He also became Pope due to the strong will of Marozia and he was somewhat a puppet in the hands of this powerful woman. Marozia hoped to see her son John on the throne, and wanted to put an end to the feudal anarchy in Rome by creating a strong civil power that would nullify the temporal power of the popes. Her error was using the popes as puppets; her son, Alberico, however did not fall into the same error and operated in the midst of political awareness, limiting the popes to only undertake religious activities. Not much is known about Stephen VII. He gave great privileges to certain monasteries. He died in February 931 and is buried in the Vatican Grottoes at Saint Peter's Basilica.

125 – **JOHN XI** (931-935). Thanks to the intrigues of his mother, Marozia, he was elected Pope during the first months of 931, when he was little over twenty years old. After being widowed by Guido of Tuscany, Marozia married his brother Hugo, King of Italy, who was just as corrupt and ambitious as she was. Together, with the consensus of John XI, they became the tyranny of Rome. Marozia's son by her first husband, Alberico II, and Alberico of Spoleto, brought the people against Marozia and Hugo, and had themselves declared prince and senator, putting an end to Marozia's aspirations to control the papacy in Rome and Italy. Even John was sent to prison by Alberico, where he died in 935. He is buried in Saint John in Lateran.

126 – **LEO VII** (936-939). A Benedictine monk, he was born in Rome and was hand picked by Alberico II. Under Leo's pontificate, Alberico II reconciled with King Hugo of Italy thanks to the peacemaking efforts of Odo of Cluny. Hugo, in exile, had tried to win back Rome by force and favoured monastic reform.

Leo VII supported him in these projects and had the abbacy of Saint Paul's, the monasteries of Sant'Agnese and Sant'Andrea, as well as those in Subiaco and Nepi rebuilt.

Leo died in July of the year 939, and his remains are in Saint Peter's Basilica.

127 – **STEPHEN VIII** (939-942). A Roman priest and titular of Saint Martino ai Monti. He also suffered under the strong political pressure of Alberico II, but he did enjoy independence in spiritual matters during his pontificate.

He continued the works of Saint Odo of Cluny's monastic reform in Italy and in Lorraine. He also worked to persuade the French barons to recognize Ludwig IV as their sovereign King, by threatening to excommunicate them if they did not. He died during the month of October in the year 942 and was buried in the Basilica of Saint Peter's in the Vatican Grottoes.

128 – **MARINUS II** (942-946). A Roman Pope, he blindly obeyed Alberico and left pretty much all of the decision making up to him.

Not a lot is known about this particular Pope. He is recognized for his spiritual governing of the Church and for continuing the reform of the monastic orders. He conceded privileges and benefits to the monasteries of Montecassino and Fulda. In these years, central Italy was going through a difficult period under the tyrannical government of King Hugo. Marinus II died during spring of the year 946 and was buried in Saint Peter's in the Vatican Grottoes.

129 – **AGAPETUS II** (946-955). Roman born, he is at the centre of several important political changes that were taking place in Italy and Europe. In 950, Lothair died and King Berenger of Italy wanted that his son marry Adelaide, Lothair's widow.

Adelaide decided to marry Otto I, who then had himself elected King of Italy, reducing Berenger to a simple vassal. In Rome, Alberico II ruled until his death in 954. Before his death, he asked the Pope that the next successor on the pontifical throne be his son Octavian. Agapetus did not have the disposition for political intrigue and fighting, so he did nothing to slow the ascent of Octavian. He was buried in Saint John in Lateran.

130 – **JOHN XII** (955-964). He was born in Rome. Octavian, Alberico's son, was elected Pope at a very young age. His immoderate lifestyle was not much adapted for life as pontiff. He asked Otto I to help him against Berenger II, crowning him Emperor in 962 and giving him back the right to confirm papal elections, in recognition. To relieve himself of Otto's domination, he tried to side with Adalberto who was Berenger II's son, but Otto made a dash to Rome and called a synod that decided against John who was substituted by Leo VIII. When Otto returned to Germany, John XII took advantage of his absence return to Rome, punishing his enemies and antipope Leo. He is buried in Saint John in Lateran.

131 – **LEO VIII** (963-965). Considered by many as an antipope, Leo VIII was elected at the request of Otto I in November 963, to substitute John XII. Otto had deposed John because of his corrupt ways and for lack of submission to the Emperor's will. After Otto I left, John XII took the throne back and Leo VIII had to escape to Camerino. On the death of John XII, Pope Benedict V was elected by the Roman people, but Otto did not recognize him. In an open dare he took away the Roman people's elective rights. Leo VIII was confirmed as Pope by Otto. He is buried in the Vatican Grottoes.

132 – **BENEDICT V** (964-966). He was born in Rome. A very erudite man, a Cardinal-deacon, Benedict was elected by the clergy and the Roman people on the death of John XII, as an act of defiance towards Emperor Otto I. In the meantime, the Emperor elected Leo VIII and did not ratify Benedict's election. When he arrived in Rome, Otto called the Vatican council, presided over by Leo VIII, which accused Benedict V. He was reduced to the level of deacon and condemned to exile in Germany. He died in 965 and his remains were brought to Rome with honour and are kept in the Vatican Grottoes.

133 – **JOHN XIII** (965-972). He was born in Rome. Bishop of Narni, he was elected nearly two months after his predecessor died. He immediately found himself involved in a complicated battle between the imperial factions and the Roman people, as well as part of the Roman nobility. His unpopularity grew so tangibly that he was forced to escape and ask refuge from Count Pandolfo of Capua in December 965. He returned to Rome nearly one year later bringing Otto I, who would remain for many years to protect him. Otto also managed to create an apparent reconciliation between the Church of the East and the West by marrying his son Otto II to the Greek princess Theophano. He was buried in Saint Paul's Outside the Walls.

134 – **BENEDICT VI** (973-974). Roman born, he was elected immediately following the death of his predecessor, but imperial confirmation arrived much later, even though the Emperor had pushed for his election. At the death of Otto I, in 973, Otto II's rise to the throne brought about strong anti-imperial feelings. Benedict VI had been supported by the Emperor and was seen as siding with the enemy, therefore he was put in prison. The first time he was imprisoned by a rich fief owner Crescenzi and the second time by a French deacon who declared himself Pope with the name Boniface VII during June of the year 974. One month afterwards, Benedict was strangled while imprisoned in Castel Sant'Angelo. He was buried in the Vatican Grottoes.

135 – **BENEDICT VII** (974-983). After the death of Benedict VI, it was the counts of Tusculum, of the imperial line, to establish order in Rome; it wasn't easy to find a papal successor, but it was finally decided that the Bishop of Sutri take the papal throne with the name Benedict VII. Roman born from the family of the Tusculum counts, he was close to the Emperor and to the Roman aristocrats. In 981, e invoked the Lateran council in which he drew up several mandates to condemn and repress simony. He tried with all his might to elevate the spiritual level of the clergy and the Church. The following July, Benedict VII died and was buried in the Roman Basilica of Holy Cross in Jerusalem.

136 – **JOHN XIV** (983-984). Otto II designated that the successor of Benedict VII, would be his own chancellor Pietro di Campanova who took the name John XIV. In December 983, Otto II, who was barely twenty-eight, suddenly died. At his death, the ambitious Henry of Bavaria immediately took the title of King of Germany; the actual heir of Otto II was only three years old and under the regency of his mother Theophano.

The fall of John XIV was fast because Constantinople reinstated antipope Boniface VII, who commited a series of horrible and violent acts against his enemies. John XIV, closed in Castel Sant'Angelo, was killed by poisoning. He is buried in the Vatican Grottoes.

137 – **JOHN XV** (985-996). Roman by birth, John VI became Pope between September and October 985 by choice of the imperial faction. The Roman noble family, Crescenzi, grew stronger and more powerful. John XI tried to free himself of their influence by granting many titles to family and friends, which greatly angered the nobility and the clergy. The Pope was forced to escape and to ask the help of Otto III, but right before Otto arrived in Rome, where John XV was waiting to crown him Emperor, the Pope died and was buried in Saint Peter's Basilica.

138 – **GREGORY V** (996-999). Bruno of Carinthia, the chaplain of the Emperor Otto II's court, was the first Pope of German nationality. His rigid character and his nationality made unpopular with the Romans, a reaction that Giovanni Crescenzi II encouraged. Gregory V was forced to leave Rome and was substituted by antipope John XVI. Otto III, who had been crowned as Emperor by Gregory V, came to his aid. The Romans consigned the antipope to Otto and Crescenzi and his followers were brought to justice. The premature death of Gregory in 999 was a suspected homicide. He is buried in Saint Peter's Basilica.

139 – **SYLVESTER II** (999-1003). Gerbert of Aurillac was the first French Pope. Born of humble origins, he was an extremely cultured man. Sylvester II worked to bring forth the ecclesiastical reform initiated by Gregory V, his predecessor. Otto III, settled upon the Aventine Hill in Rome, assuming the role of papal defender. Together they were supposed to have brought peace back to the world and guide the people on the road to God in the new millennium. But an insurgence by the people and the Roman nobility forced Otto to leave Rome. He fled together with the Pope in 1001. The following January, Otto died and in May of 1003 Pope Sylvester died. He is buried in the Basilica of Saint John in Lateran.

140 – **JOHN XVII** (1003). Very little is known about the popes who followed Sylvester II and were elected by Rome's new leader Giovanni Crescenzi II. Chaos had reigned in Rome during the last months of Sylvester II's pontificate. Power was nearly completely in the hands of Giovanni Crescenzi, the son of the legendary hero Crescenzi who died in Castel Sant' Angelo. John XVII, of the noble Sicconi family, lived a very brief pontificate and died a short six months after his election. He is buried in Rome in the Basilica of Saint John in Lateran.

141 – **JOHN XVIII** (1004-1009). This Roman was elected at the request of the Crescenzi family, whom he allowed to strongly influence his decisions. He favoured missionary works during his reign and relations with the Eastern Church were serene. In 1004, Henry II of Bavaria came to Italy and was crowned King of Italy in Verona by the Archbishop of Milan. A rebellion followed, in Pavia, to which Henry responded by sacking and burning the city. John did not intervene in the terrible situation. He conceded various benefits to Benedictine monasteries, the same order to which he belonged before being crowned as Pope. He died in July of 1009, while he was at the Abbey of Saint Paul's.

142 – **SERGIUS IV** (1009-1012). He was born in Rome. His name was Peter, and he was the Bishop of Albano before he was consecrated as Pope thanks to the support of the Crescenzi family. He did many things during his pontificate; he was interested in the good of the Church and elevating the behaviour of the clergy. When the Sainted Sepulchre was sacked by the Egyptian Caliph, Sergius IV began promoting the crusades. He wrote that all of the Christians should seek to vindicate themselves, but his call to arms was in vain. He died in May of the year 1012, and is buried in the Basilica of Saint John in Lateran.

143 – **BENEDICT VIII** (1012-1024). Theophylactus, from the family of the counts of Tusculum, was elected Benedict VIII against the candidate of the antagonistic Crescenzi family, who countered with antipope Gregory. Benedict asked Henry II to help out against the antipope. Two years later, in Rome, he crowned Henry as Emperor. Benedict called a council in Pavia in the year 1018 where he officially condemned simony, duels, and ecclesiastical concubines. He was able to successfully push back the Saracens who had arrived in Tuscany and he also blocked the Greek advancement in the South. He died in 1024 and is buried in Saint Peter's Basilica.

144 – **JOHN XIX** (1024-1032). His name was Romano and he also descended from the family of the counts of Tusculum. He was Benedict VIII's brother and during his pontificate he had been elected as senator and put at the head of the temporal government of the Church. After Henry II died in Germany, Conrad II, "*the Salian,*" was elected King in 1024. In Saint Peter's, John XIX crowned him as Emperor in 1027, to help maintain relations with the German empire. John XIX protected Guido d'Arezzo, the Benedictine monk that invented the new notes of the musical scale. He died in 1032 and was buried in Saint Peter's Basilica.

145/147/150 – **BENEDICT IX** (1032 -1048). Elected Pope as a very young man, Benedict IX was supported by the family of the counts of Tusculum. Highly devoted to Conrad II, he followed the imperialistic vein of his family and obeyed the Emperor's request to excommunicate Heribert, the Archbishop of Milan. In 1044, Benedict IX was forced to flee the power of the antagonistic Crescenzi family who replaced him with Sylvester III. The next year, Benedict returned to the throne, to leave a short time later, this time due to an exchange of money with Gregory VI. He was put on the throne a third time in 1047 for eight months and then he finally retired to a monastery in Grottaferrata, where he died and was buried around 1050.

146 – **SYLVESTER III** (January 20-February 10, 1045). Between the end of 1044 and the beginnings of the next year, a rebellion caused Benedict IX to flee. The Romans declared that they had had enough of the corrupt Pope and with the help of the Crescenzi family; he was elected in place of Sylvester III. Only twenty days later, when Benedict IX, returned, helped by of the counts of Tusculum, Sylvester had to escape and find refuge in the Sabine area. It is thought that later he was authorized to keep his diocese, but nothing else is known about his life.

148 – **GREGORY VI** (1045-1046). Giovanni Graziano became Pope and took the name Gregory VI. He, like Sylvester III, can be considered an antipope, because the deposing of Benedict IX is questionable, because there was an exchange of money for an ecclesiastical position of great power. Gregory VI was a man of great religiosity and good intentions. He met Henry III, who followed Conrad II as King of Germany. But, Henry called the council of Sutri in December 1046, deposing Sylvester III and Gregory VI and recognizing them guilty of simony. Gregory was forced to abdicate. He was exiled to France to the abbey of Cluny, where he died.

149 – **CLEMENT II** (1046-1047). On December 23, 1046 Henry III held another council in Rome, in which Benedict IX was judged in absentia for not being present. The King chose a new Saxon Pope, the Bishop of Bamberg named Suidger, who took the name Clement II. A few days after this, he crowned Henry II as Emperor in Saint Peter's. In this way securing the dominion of the pontifical throne by taking the power away from the feudal lay. Clement was very active. He led a council against simony; he resolved a difference between the bishops of Milan and Ravenna and the Patriarch of Ravenna. He died in Germany just a year after his election and was buried in Bamberg in a very grandiose sarcophagus in the Duomo.

151 – **DAMASUS II** (1048). Poppone was born in Bavaria from the Baragneri family. He was Bishop of Brixen and he was elected Pope in July 1048, following the renouncement of Aliardo, the Bishop of Lions on behalf of Emperor Henry III of Germany. Damasus II died of malaria in Palestrina just 24 hours after his election. He was buried in Rome in the Basilica of Saint Lorenzo Outside the Walls

152 – **Saint LEO IX** (1049-1054). Born to an Alsatian noble family, his former name was Brunone. He was elected by the clergy and the Roman people in free elections. He called several synods, to enforce ecclesiastic celibacy and to combat simony and heresy. He was not able to win the battle against the Normans, who began the pontifical feudal investiture of the reign of Naples. During his pontificate the doctrinal and political contrast began with the Church of the East. Just three months after his death, in 1054, the definitive schism between the Greek Church and the Latin Church took place. He is buried in Saint Peter's Basilica in the left transept.

153 – **VICTOR II** (1055-1057). Born in Bavaria, Gebhard of the family of the counts of Tollenstein- Hirschberg, was elected one year after the death of Leo IX, supported by Emperor Henry III. He remained faithful to the Emperor, and even served as the caretaker of Henry III's son after his death. He continued the works of reforming the Church that had been started by his predecessor.

He worked to help Godfrey of Lorraine re-establish his power in southern Italy. He nominated his brother Frederick as Cardinal. Victor died in the city of Arezzo during 1057, and was buried in Rome in the Church of Saint Mary in Cosmedin.

154 – **STEPHEN IX (X)** (1057-1058). Brother of Duke Goffredo, his name was Frederick of Lorraine. Chancellor of the pontifical court he was directed to work with the Greek Church towards establishing peace between the two. He surrounded himself with illustrious men such as Saint Peter Damian and Cardinal Hildebrand, who would later become Gregory VII. He died just a few months after his pontificate began, after him there was a brief reign by antipope Benedict X. With the death of Stephen IX, the series of five German popes that had begun with Clement II came to an end. He is buried in Florence in the Duomo.

155 – **NICHOLAS II** (1059-1061). Born in Bourgogne, Gerard of Burgundy was the Bishop of Florence when he was elected as Pope in opposition to antipope Benedict X. He was elected thanks to the pressure of the Roman nobility who were trying to win back their lost authority in pontifical elections.

The antipope was deposed in the council of Sutri. Right after being consecrated, Nicholas called the council of Lateran, which defined certain provisions regarding discipline and faith; he emanated a decree reforming the procedures used in pontifical elections. He died in Florence and is buried in the Duomo.

156 – **ALEXANDER II** (1061-1073). Born of a noble family from Milan, Anselm of Baggio was elected Pope with the support of Hildebrand of Soana, who with the support of the Normans would later become Gregory VII. Regent Empress Agnes, for the young Henry IV of Germany, opposed his election and had Honorius II elected as antipope at the council of Basle. Alexander II was confirmed as Pope in 1062 at the diet of Augsburg. He dedicated himself mostly to religious activities and renewed the decrees against clergy practicing simony and clergy keeping concubines and he worked towards establishing collaboration between the lay people and the clergy. He died in Rome and is buried in the Vatican Grottoes.

157 – **Saint GREGORY VII** (1073-1085). Hildebrand of Soana was elected Pope by unanimous vote. Gregory's policies posed the problem of the long standing difficulty between the pontificate and the Empire, referred to as the "battle of investiture." Famous for his relationship with the German Emperor Henry IV, who was excommunicated in Canossa in 1076 for his hostile attitude towards the pontiff and was forced to humiliate himself for absolution. Henry IV however fought back by electing an antipope, Clement III, who crowned him Emperor in Rome in the year 1084. Gregory VII had to flee to Salerno where he died in May of 1085. He was made Saint by Paul V in 1606 and he is buried in the Church of Saint Matthew in Salerno.

158 – **Blessed VICTOR III** (1086-1087). From the family of the Lombard Dukes of Benevento he was the abbot of Montecassino, when he was elected against his own wishes. It was Gregory VII that wanted him to become Pope and Victor continued his policies. He excommunicated Henry IV once again, overturned elections for simony, condemned the lay investiture, and excommunicated antipope Clement III during the synod of Benevento.

He died while he was in Montecassino and is buried in the monastery there. He was declared Blessed in 1887, by Leo XIII.

159 – **Blessed URBAN II** (1088-1099). Of noble origins, Odo of Lagery entered the Benedictine order in 1076. After being elected Pope, he undertook reforming the Church as well as the battle against lay meddling in the ecclesiastical sphere.

He was an expert on canonical law and he followed a strategy of diplomatic action aimed at isolating Henry IV. He was able to reinforce the authority of the pontificate over the bishops and only in 1094 was he able to return to Rome. His name is tied to the first Crusades which were undertaken to free the holy land from the Turks. He died in 1099 just a few days after Jerusalem was taken. Since 1881 he has been venerated as Blessed. He is buried in the Vatican Grottoes.

160 – **PASCHAL II** (1099-1118). The monk Rainerus of Blera was born in Ravenna. He was elected Pope against three antipope antagonists: Theodore, Albert and Sylvester IV. He fought in the war over the investiture against Henry IV and his son Henry V. He accepted a truce with Henry V in Sutri on 1111, but because the agreement was unfavourable towards the Church, in the council of Lateran the following year, Paschal II annulled it. When the Henry V arrived in Italy, the Pope was forced to escape to Benevento. When he returned to Rome with the help of the Normans, he died just a few days later. He is buried in the Basilica of Saint John in Lateran.

161 – **GELASIUS II** (1118-1119). He was born in Gaeta. A Benedictine monk, Giovanni Caetani was also chancellor of the Church. His election happened in secrecy at the Palatine. As soon as the conclave was finished, he was arrested by Cencius Frangipane, head of the partisans of Henry V. Liberated by the Roman people, he was forced by Henry V to flee to Gaeta and the Emperor declared another Pope with the name Gregory VIII. Gelasius excommunicated the Emperor and returned to Rome the moment he left. He was soon forced to leave by the Frangipane troops, so he escaped and fled to Cluny where he died and is buried.

162 – **CALLISTUS II** (1119-1124). Guido of Burgundy was the papal legate in France and the Bishop of Vienna. In Cluny, he was elected Pope in 1119 and during the same year at the council at Reims he excommunicated Henry V. Once he resolved the problems with the imperial antipope Gregory VIII, he reached an agreement with the Emperor stipulating the edict of Worms in 1122, which recognized the Emperor's temporal investiture, leaving the bishops and the Church with spiritual power. In 1123 he called the first Lateran the council in which 25 canons were sanctioned to repress abuses and to help the new crusade. At that time the second crusade began. Callistus II is buried in Saint John in Lateran.

163 – **HONORIUS II** (1124-1130). He was born in Bologna. Lambert Scannabecchi was one of the negotiators of the Concorde of Worms. He was elected Pope by the Frangipane faction, and was favoured by the Emperor. He managed to win against antipope Celestine II and reigned peacefully. He sustained Lothair of Saxony who succeeded Henry V.
During his pontificate, Italy saw the rise of the Guelphi faction, sustainers of the Pope, and the Ghibelline faction, who were sustainers of the Emperor. He approved the Templar Order and participated in coordinating the basis for the Holy War. He died in the monastery of Saint Gregory al Celio. He is buried in the Basilica of Saint John in Lateran.

164 – **INNOCENT II** (1130-1143). He was born in Rome. On the death of Honorius II, the Cardinal Gregory Papereschi was proclaimed pontiff. He was also elected with the support of the Frangipane faction against antipope Anacletus II, who was backed by the Pierleoni family. Anacletus II took Rome with the help of the potent Norman Ruggero II, forcing Innocent II to flee for long periods of time. With the help of Saint Bernard of Chiaravalle and of Lothair, the German Emperor and successor of Henry, he called the second Lateran council which brought and end to the schism in 1139. He is buried in the Roman Church of Saint Mary in Trastevere.

165 – **CELESTINE II** (1143-1144). Guido de Castellisi succeeded Innocent II in a period of turmoil caused by the heretical preaching of Arnold of Brescia. With the help of Saint Bernard he tried to resolve conflicts within the Church, but with poor results; however he did manage to alleviate the warring status between Scotland and England. He was Pope for only four months and he was buried in Lateran. From this Pope began the so-called "*Prophecies of Saint Malachi*" of the Archbishop of Armagh in Ireland.

166 – **LUCIUS II** (1144-1145). Gerard Caccianemici was born in Bologna to a humble family. When he was elected Pope the situation in Rome continued to be difficult. The Senatorial party influenced the climate heavily. The government and the Senate were led by Giordano Pierleoni, brother of antipope Anacletus II. They declared that the temporal power of the popes had ended and the city founded a constitutional republic. Lucius II tried to react, but during the turmoil in the battles that followed, he was hit by a rock and died a few days later. He is buried in Lateran.

167 – **Blessed EUGENE III** (1145-1153). Bernard Paganelli of Pisa was a Cistercian abbot. He was elected Pope during a time of great time of turmoil filled with autonomous movements, and for this he was forced to leave Rome. In 1145 he managed to bring about the second crusade obtaining the support of Saint Bernard of Chiaravalle who later dedicated him the ascetic piece: "*De consideration*." He managed to return to Rome after lengthy negotiations with Frederick Barbarossa.He died a short time later in 1153. Pius IX declared him Blessed in 1872. He is buried in Saint John in Lateran.

168 – **ANASTASIUS IV** (1153-1154). When Conrad Suburra was elected Pope he was already quite advanced in age and had little interest in political matters. For this reason he counted on Cardinal Breakspear, who would later become Adrian IV, to operate as his chancellor. He did much in the areas of charity and public assistance, and he managed in part to obtain peace within the Church. He confirmed the order of the Cavaliers of Malta and restored the Pantheon. He was generous with Rome, which had been hit by a wave of poverty and for this reason he is referred to as "*Father of Rome and Apostle of Charity.*" He is buried in Saint John in Lateran.

169 – **ADRIAN IV** (1154-1159). Nicholas Breakspear was born in London and still today remains the only English Pope. From the moment his papacy began, he energetically countered the rebellion that had been provoked by Arnold of Brescia. Paying his debts for assistance given, he crowned Frederick Barbarossa as Emperor in Saint Peter's. Arnold was condemned to burn at the stake by Pope Adrian who then threw the heretic's ashes in the Tiber River. Differences of opinion with Barbarossa led Adrian to support the new Norman King William I, conceding the reign of Sicily to him. He is buried in the Basilica of Saint Peter's.

170 – **ALEXANDER III** (1159-1181). Roland Bandinelli of Siena was a famous theologian. His pontificate was characterized by the many battles that he brought against Frederick Barbarossa. The Emperor responded by pitting four different antipopes against him. A schism began, but Alexander firmly opposed them by asking help from various European states. In 1160 he excommunicated Barbarossa. He supported the Lombardy Union, which defeated the Emperor in Legnano during the year 1176. Frederick was humiliated in front of the Pope and accepted the Venetian peace treaty. In 1179 Alexander III called the third Lateran council. He was severe in his condemnation of corruption and in defending the rights of the Church. He is buried in the Basilica of Saint John in Lateran.

171 – **LUCIUS III** (1181-1185). Ubaldus Allucingolus of Lucca was elected Pope in Velletri, while Rome was in the hands of the Republican government controlled by followers of Arnold of Brescia. He returned to Rome two-months afterwards, but soon he was forced flee again, this time without ever being able to return, because he lost the support of Frederick Barbarossa. He went to Verona and called a council where he took measures against the Valdensian heresy by the Cathars and the Arnaldists. He is buried in the Cathedral of the Verona.

172 – **URBAN III** (1185-187). Born in Milan with the name Humbert Crivelli he was made Pope during a conclave in Verona where the pontifical court was residing, during this time of great tension with the Emperor. While he was Cardinal, it was his idea to form the Lombardy league. When he became Pope, he was a strong antagonist of Frederick and tried, without success, to stop the marriage of Frederick's son Henry to Constance of Altavilla who was the heiress to the reign of Sicily. He died in 1187, from a pain caused by the news that the Saracens had occupied Jerusalem. He is buried in the Cathedral of Ferrara.

173 – **GREGORY VIII** (25 October-17 December 1187). Alberto de Mora from Benevento was a professor of canonical law at the University of Bologna. Once elected Pope, he immediately went to Pisa to reconcile the people of the city with the people of Genoa. He worked towards the organization of the third crusade, in the meantime helping Christians in the Holy Land, who were oppressed by the Saracens. He began peace negotiations with Frederick Barbarossa, by whom he was much esteemed. This probably would have had a positive outcome if Gregory had not died only 57 days after his election. He is buried in the Cathedral in Pisa.

174 – **CLEMENT III** (1187-1191). Paul Scolari, Cardinal and Bishop of Palestrina, once elected managed to make peace with the Roman Senate and to return the pontificate to Rome, 60 years after it had been forced to move. He resided in Rome undisturbed. He began the third crusade in which they Italian Marine Republics participated. Philip II of France, Richard the lion hearted of England and Frederick Barbarossa all died during that crusade. At the end of it, Clement obtained a piece of coastland in Palestine and permission to visit the Sainted Sepulchre, which had been in the hands of Sultan Saladin since 1187. Clement III died in Rome, during the year 1191 and is buried in Lateran.

175 – **CELESTINE III** (1191-1198). Born in Rome to the Orsini family, Hyacinth Bobo, was a valiant diplomat and had been the pontifical legate in Spain, France, and to Frederick Barbarossa. He was elected Pope when he was already advanced in age; in fact he was 85 years old. He immediately crowned Henry VI as Emperor, Frederick's son, but did try to check his targeting of the Sicilian throne by supporting Tancredi of Altavilla. He believed in the unbreakable bonds of matrimony. He approved the German military order and was in favour of the Templars. After many popes that had been forced to live outside Italy, Celestine III was the first to spend his entire pontificate in Rome. He is buried in Lateran.

176 – **INNOCENT III** (1198-1216). At the time, Lothair of the Counts of Segni was gifted with a strong character, great intelligent and a strong political sense. He was elected Pope at only 38 years of age. Innocent did everything in his power to re-establish the papal strength in the pontifical states and to save the unity with the Church in the East, trying to establish peace among all Christians. The heretics and the Byzantine Church were opposed to that unity. To reaffirm spiritual values, he approved the mendicant orders of the Dominicans and the Franciscans. He called the fourth Lateran council, in which he called the fourth crusade was ordered to try and resolve the schism of the East. He supported Frederick II of Swabia who was elected King of Germany in 1212. He is buried in Lateran.

177 - **HONORIUS III** (1216-1227). Born in Rome, his name was Cencius Savelli. Once elected Pope, he continued the works of his predecessor. To ensure his support when he called the fifth crusade, in 1220 he crowned Frederick II as Emperor. Frederick did not leave for the Holy Land, but he did sustain and support the Church in the battle against heresy, together with the King of Aragon and Louis VIII of France, who took back up the Albigensian crusade and instituted the tribunals of the Inquisition. Honorius III approved the Dominicans and in 1223 the Franciscan brothers founded by Francis of Assisi. He is buried in Saint Mary Major.

178 - **Blessed GREGORY IX** (1227-1241). At that time Ugolino dè Conti, Count of Segni, made Cardinal in 1198, was the Bishop of Ostia. He backed Saint Dominique and was friends with Saint Francis. He ordained the order of the Clarisse. He became Pope and excommunicated Frederick II for not respecting his promise to finish the crusade and he excommunicated him once again in 1239 when Frederick II reinforced the centralized state, threatening the privileges of the Church. The war came to a quick end with the triumph of the Ghibellines. Gregory IX canonized Francis of Assisi, Antonio of Padova and Dominique of Guzman. He had a sincere and strong religious sentiment, at times this made him too severe and he is remembered for the instituting the tribunal of the Inquisition. He is buried in the Vatican.

179 - **CELESTINE IV** (28 October-10 November 1241). Born in Milan, Godfrey Castiglioni was elected Pope by a conclave that was composed of ten cardinals who were not able to choose the new Pope until they were closed and locked inside the Septizonium Palace on Celio Hill. From this time the terminology conclave derives from the Latin term "*cum clave.*" He approved the order of Dominicans and Franciscans. He prohibited the clergy from playing cards. However, Celestine IV's pontificate passed like a meteor, he died only 17 days after his election without ever having received the papal triple reign. He is buried in the Vatican Grottoes.

180 - **INNOCENT IV** (1243-1254). Born in Genova, Sinibaldo de' Fieschi was elected Pope in Anagni after twenty months of the pontifical throne remaining empty because of the hostility created over the conclave of Frederick II. This Pope affirmed the dominance of the Papacy as the wellspring of every right in the Empire and he confirmed the excommunication of Frederick II. Due to the battle between the Emperor and the Pope, the pontiff had to leave Rome and was only able to return after 1250, the year that Frederick II died. Four years later Frederick II's son also died, Conrad IV, who in turn left his son, Corradino, under the tutelage of the pontiff. He was buried in the Cathedral of San Gennaro in Naples.

181 - **ALEXANDER IV** (1254-1261). Born in Anagni, Renaldo of the counts of Segni was the nephew of Gregory IX and in the footsteps of his predecessors he had many quarrels with Manfredi and Corradino; he was unable to place the Guelph Charles d' Anjou on the throne of the reign of Naples and Sicily. In religious areas he condemned the "flagellants" (men that stripped to their waist, covered their heads with a hat and carried "*staffile*"), and the heretics. He favoured the monastic orders; he canonized Saint Claire and gave support to missionary works. When Rome became insecure for him he left and went to Viterbo. He died there and was buried in the Duomo.

182 - **URBAN IV** (1261-1264). The Guelphs and the Ghibellines divided Rome and a large part of other Italian cities. Amidst the many difficulties, the Frenchman Jacques Pantalèon, Patriarch of Jerusalem, was elected as Pope; he happened to be in Rome for his ministry. He immediately contrasted the power of the Svevi of Sicily who had gained importance after the victory of Montaperti on behalf of Manfredi. He supported, on the other hand, the brother of Louis of France, Charles of Anjou and he negotiated to let him conquer the reign of Sicily. Urban IV instituted the feast of Corpus Domini in 1264 and Saint Thomas d' Aquinas composed the prayers. He is buried in the Cathedral of Deruta (Perugia).

183 - **CLEMENT IV** (1265-1268). Born in France, Guy Foulques had a military and law background. Secretary of Louis IX, he took the sacred orders on the death of his wife. Clement IV, as Pope, continued the anti-Sveva policy concerning the investiture of Charles d' Anjou in the reign of Sicily. He contrasted the arrival of Corradino in Italy, where he was decapitated. With Charles d' Anjou having defeated Manfredi's troops (Manfredi died in battle). Once the Sveva domination had ended the French tyranny began. Clement reinforced the Inquisition and protected Ruggero Bacone. He is buried in the Dominican Church in Viterbo.

184 - **Blessed GREGORY X** (1271-1276). Born in Piacenza, Tebaldo Visconti was elected Pope after the longest conclave in the history of the Church; it lasted three whole years. Tebaldo was a layman, he was called back from the Holy Land, where he lived. He was first ordained as a priest and crowned as pontiff the next year. Once he became Pope he tried to establish provisional measures to reduce the length of conclave, by establishing standards for the elections of the popes. His pontificate was characterized by his perfect impartiality in trying to bring peace back to the world. He supported the election of the German Emperor Rudolph of Hapsburg. He called the council at Lions in 1274. He was declared Blessed by Clement XI in 1713. He is buried in the Duomo of Arezzo.

185 - **Blessed INNOCENT V** (21 January-22 June 1276). Peter of Tarantasio, French and of the Savoy family, studied in Paris at the school of Thomas d' Aquinas. He was a great theologian and philosopher, in fact he was known as "doctor famosissimus." He was the right hand man of Gregory X and on his death Innocent was elected Pope by unanimous vote. In only five months of pontificate he acted with wisdom to help maintain peace in Italy. In fact he managed to pacify many troubled relations: between Pisa and the Tuscan cities and between Genoa and Charles d' Anjou. He began to organize a crusade. The people venerated him as a Saint and then Leo XIII proclaimed him blessed. He was buried in Lateran.

186 - **ADRIAN V** (11 July-18 August 1276). Ottobono Fieschi, Born in Genoa, died just one month after his election in Viterbo, even before he had been officially crowned as Pope. He was elected with the support of Charles d' Anjou. In recognition, Adrian immediately annulled the changes made by Gregory X regarding the regulation of the conclave. He intended to substitute the rules with a new constitution but he didn't have time because of his early death. He regulated the ecclesiastical orders. He is buried in Viterbo in the Church of Saint Francis.

187 - **JOHN XXI** (1276-1277). Pietro di Giuliano was born in Lisbon and was erroneously elected Pope with the name John XXI, because a John XX had never been proclaimed. He was a famous doctor, but not a real expert in political or religious affairs, for this reason he left those matters to Cardinal Giovanni Caetani Orsini, the future Nicholas III. He continued his studies and wrote many scientific and philosophical documents. The most famous of his writings is the logic manual, "*Summulae logicales.*" He died when the room he was staying at in Viterbo crumbled upon him. He is buried in the Cathedral of Saint Laurence in Viterbo.

188 - **NICHOLAS III** (1277-1280). Giovanni Caetani Orsini was Roman and was elected Pope for his long experience and his cultural level, after a conclave which lasted six months. He espoused the politics of balance, in which the Church had a hegemonic role. He also worked to limit the excessive power of Charles d' Anjou and favoured the marriage between his nephew Charles Martel and Clementia the daughter of Rudolph of Hapsburg, from whom he gained ample rights in Romagna. He was a Pope famous for nepotism, and is remembered by Dante in his *"Inferno."* He had the first building of the Vatican constructed and is buried in the Vatican Grottoes.

189 - **MARTIN IV** (1281-1285). After six months without a Pope, the cardinals who were on the side of Charles d' Anjou managed to get Frenchman Simon de Brie elected. He immediately began a reciprocal relationship with Angioini.
He supported Charles even after the Sicilian people rose against him in 1282, wanting the Aragon dominion known as the *Sicilian Vespers*. He was not well-liked in Rome, in fact he lived in Orvieto, Perugia and Montefiascone. He was accused of having frequently used his spiritual sanctions to resolve political problems. Dante placed him in *"Purgatorio,"* among the greedy. He is buried in the Cathedral of Perugia.

190 - **HONORIUS IV** (1285-1287). Giacomo Savelli, born in Rome, was elected pontiff after only four days of conclave and his first act of office was to bring order back to the pontifical state. He tried to settle differences in the spirit of Christian brotherhood. He governed with moderation and justice, together with his brother Pandolfo who in those years was a senator in Rome. He introduced the study of Oriental languages to the University of Paris. He gave the final approval to the order of Carmelites, took great care with the religious orders and was a supporter of missionaries. He is buried in the Basilica of Saint Mary in Aracoelis.

191 - **NICHOLAS IV** (1288-1292). He was born in Disciano d'Ascoli. The first Franciscan Pope, Girolamo Masci was elected after nearly a year without a Pope. In Rome he was given the title of senator for life, but he was accused by the people and the nobility of too heavily favouring the Colonna family. He was forced to leave Rome for various upheavals. He crowned Charles II d' Anjou as King of Sicily in 1289 and favoured his first born Charles Martel for the throne of Hungary. He favoured the missions in Persia and China, and among the Mongolians and the Tartars. He is responsible for the mosaics in the Basilica of Santa Mary Major and Saint John. He is buried in Saint Mary Major.

192 - **Saint CELESTINE V** (5 July-13 December 1294). He was born in Isernia. Pietro del Murrone, having found the Benedictine order spiritually lacking and deluded by the experience, he retired to the Grottoes of Monte Murrone near Sulmona. There he created a community of Benedictine hermits, which was approved in 1263. Pietro was elected Pope with the desire to bring a strong spiritual renewal to the Church. Fairly soon however, he left and decided to renounce the throne, possibly due to pressures by Cardinal Caetani, who later became Boniface VIII. Caetani confined him to the castle of Fumone where he died in 1296. He was canonized by Clement V in 1313 and is buried in the Church of Collemaggio in Aquila.

193 - **BONIFACE VIII** (1294-1303). Benedict Caetani, of noble Roman origins was without a doubt one of the most authoritarian popes of the medieval period. He was a man of great culture and possibilities and he was a strong believer in the supremacy of the Church. Famous for his battle with Philip the Fair, King of France, which can be considered the last phase of the grandiose duel between the papacy and the Empire of the medieval period. A memorable moment during the pontificate of Boniface VIII was the celebration, during the year 1300, of the first jubilee in history of the Church. Dante places him amidst those guilty of simony in his "*Inferno*." He is buried in the Vatican Grottoes.

194 - **Blessed BENEDICT XI** (1303-1304). Nicholas of Boccasini, born in Treviso, was a Dominican. He was a Pope with a peaceful nature and mild character. He made peace with Cardinal Colonna, who had been excommunicated by Boniface VIII, but was inflexible with Nogaret and Sciarra Colonna for the attempts at Anagni. He revoked the canonical censures against Philip IV the Fair, in the name of peace. He tried to intervene in the internal politics of Florence by supporting the Bianchi faction. He wrote sermons and some comments on passages in the Book of John, the Psalms and the Apocalypse. He was declared Blessed in 1783. He is buried in Perugia in the Church of San Domenico.

195 - **CLEMENT V** (1305-1314). Bertrand de Gott, born in France, was elected Pope with a compromise between the Italian cardinals and Philip the Fair. Clement V always felt the strong and decisive influence of the French King. On the wishes of Philip, in 1309, he transferred the papal seat from Rome to Avignon, accepted to overturn the Papal Bulls of Boniface VIII and decided to suppress the order of Templars; assuming all of their riches. Clement was interested in culture; in fact he created the studies of Oriental languages in Paris, Bologna, Salamanca, the University of Orleans and of Perugia. He is buried in France in Uzeste.

196 - **JOHN XXII** (1316-1334). Born in France in Cahors, Jacques Duèse succeeded Clement V after two years without a pontiff. He established himself in Avignon where the papal throne had been moved. Though he lived in France, he reorganized the Roman chancellery and instituted the tribunal of the Roman Rota (better known as "*Sacra Rota*"). He had an openly antagonistic relationship with Ludwig of Bavaria, around whom gathered all of John XXII's opposition, and whom the Pope excommunicated in 1327. In an open battle, Ludwig had himself proclaimed Emperor in Rome declared an antipope, with the name Nicholas V, in 1328. Later Nicholas asked for a pardon and accepted the Pope's authority. He is buried in the Cathedral of Avignon.

197 - **BENEDICT XII** (1334-1342). Another French Pope, Jacques Fournier, confirmed the papal residence in Avignon, by beginning the construction of the papal palace. He worked to change corrupt usages in the Church and to eliminate abuses, by condemning nepotism and simony.
He worked to stop the Hundred Year War between the English and the French. He also worked to towards establishing peaceful relations with Ludwig of Bavaria, but the German electorate refused papal influence in the nomination of the German King. He is buried in the Cathedral of Avignon.

198 - **CLEMENT VI** (1342-1352). Pierre Roger, a Benedictine monk and French noble-man, rose to the throne with the name Clement VI. He brought the pomp that he had learned at the court of the King of France, to the pontifical throne. His lifestyle and his blatant tendencies towards nepotism attracted a lot of criticism. He bought the City of Avignon from Queen Joanna I of Naples in 1348. Initially he backed the rebellion in Rome of the tribune Cola of Rienzo, but later due to his excesses, he excommunicated him and had him imprisoned. He established the date for the second Jubilee in 1350, and decided that it should be celebrated every 50 years. He is buried in the monastery of La Chaise-Dieu, in Haute-Loire.

199 - **INNOCENT VI** (1352-1362). Etienne Aubert was also French and resided in Avignon. He decided to restore the pontifical sovereignty to Italy, so he sent Cola of Rienzo and Cardinal Albornoz, who was his vicar. The Cardinal managed to accomplish the mission entrusted to him, on the contrary to Rienzo, killed by the Roman people, even though initially he had been welcomed triumphantly. He worked, like Benedict XII, to stop the Hundred Year War between France in England. In 1360 he settled the peace treaty of Brétigny. He asked Francesco Petrarca to serve as his secretary, but the poet refused because he loved his freedom too much and was opposed to the papacy in Avignon. He is buried in the Carthusian monastery of Villeneuve-les-Avignon.

200 - **Blessed URBAN V** (1362-1370). Born in a noble French family, he was a Benedictine monk. Guillaume de Grimoard was a pious Pope, very loved by the people and motivated by the spirit of charity. In his desire to return the papal seat to Rome, he was helped by Cardinal legate Albornoz, in 1367, against the desires of the French court and the cardinals. Unfortunately, due to the rebellion in Viterbo and Perugia, and the renewal of the hostilities between France and England, Urban V was no longer safe and had to return to Avignon, where he died three months later in sanctity. He was declared Blessed in 1870, but Pius IX and was buried in the Church of Saint Victor in Marseilles.

201 - **GREGORY XI** (1370-1378). Born in France in Maumont, Pierre Roger de Beaufort tried to return the papal throne to Rome from the very beginning of his pontificate. This was not possible due to the international climate and the internal conflicts that lacerated Italy. A rebellion occurred in the Church state of Florence, where he had to intercede.
Finally even Saint Catherine of Siena, in 1377, asked for his help. Gregory finally came to Rome where he died one year later. He is buried in the Church of Saint Francesca Romana.

202 - **URBAN VI** (1378-1389). Bartolomeo Prignano was born in Naples. During the conclave the Roman people rose up, out of fear that another French Pope might be elected. The turmoil was taken to heart by a group of dissident cardinals who reunited in Fondi and elected an antipope, Cardinal Robert of Geneva, who took the name Clement VII and established himself in Avignon. This was the beginning of the great Western schism which lasted nearly 40 years until the reign of Martin V. Urban was a man with impeccable behaviour, he was quick to anger and was nicknamed "*inurbane*", rendering himself severe even with the cardinals that supported him. He called the Jubilee in the year 1390. He is buried in the Vatican Grottoes.

203 - **BONIFACE IX** (1389-1404). Pietro Tomacelli was elected Pope during a conclave of 14 cardinals who gathered in Rome against the antagonistic antipope in Avignon. Boniface IX tried to find a compromise with Clement VII, the antipope, but during the negotiations, Clement died and Benedict XIII was elected in his place and he demonstrated himself hostile from the very beginning. Boniface celebrated two Holy years: the first in 1390, called by Urban VI and another in 1400, for the turn of the century. He tried to centralize political power and managed to reinforce papal authority. He founded the University of Ferrara. His greed for money forced him to sell many indulgences and ecclesiastical roles (to just about anyone), and this garnered harsh criticism. He is buried in the Vatican Grottoes.

204 - **INNOCENT VII** (1404-1406). Born in Sulmona, Cosimo Gentile dè Migliorati was elected Pope in Rome, while in Avignon, there was an antipope by the name Benedict XIII, with whom he intransigent. He excommunicated Ladislao of Naples with whom he had very close contacts in the beginning, but who later pushed him to war. Education was very close to his heart and with a papal bull he reorganized the University of Rome, adding additional fields of study to the curriculum. Turmoil in Rome caused him to move the papal throne to Viterbo. Later he was called back to the city by the Roman citizens and remained there until he died. He is buried in the Vatican Grottoes.

205 - **GREGORY XII** (1406-1415). Angelo Corrario was from Venice. Once elected as pontiff he did not maintain the promise that he, antipope Benedict XIII and thirteen cardinals would all step down, in the interest of resolving the conflicts of the schism. For this reason the two popes were deposed during the council of Pisa, where a third Pope was elected by name of Alexander V. The next year, due to the death of Alexander, the council elected Pope John XXIII. It was a critical time for the Church with three popes reigning simultaneously. During the council of Constance, in 1414, Sigismund, the Emperor, deposed the two antipopes and later Gregory XII decided to abdicate. He is buried in the Duomo of Recanati.

206 - **MARTIN V** (1417-1431). With the election of Odo Colonna, the pontifical throne once again hosted a Roman after 130 years. He was elected in 1417 during the 41st session of the council of Constance and his pontificate is remembered above all for his incessant efforts towards unifying of the Church. This reached its apex in 1429 when Martin obtained the renouncement of antipope Clement VIII. He also worked towards the pacification of the Church state, without ever forgetting papal supremacy. In 1423 to revive religious sentiment, he called an extraordinary Holy year where he opened the *Porta Santa* in Saint John in Lateran for the first time.

207 - **EUGENE IV** (1431-1447). Gabriel Condulmer, born in Venice, was a nephew of Gregory XII. His pontificate was made more difficult by the council of Basle, which he called in 1431. Unhappy with the council's proceedings, he disbanded it and called another in Ferrara, which he then transferred to Florence. The members of the council of Basle, however, in open opposition to Eugene, sustained the supremacy of the council over the Pope. They deposed him and elected Pope Amadeus VIII Duke of Savoy with the name Felix V, who was the last antipope in history. Eugene IV managed to return to Rome in 1443 and to make peace with the French and the German princes. He did much for the humanities and protected artists and scholars of his time, including Blessed Angelico, Pinturicchio and L.B. Alberti. He is buried in Lateran.

208 - NICHOLAS V (1447-1455). At the election of Cardinal Tommaso Parentucelli the council of Basle was still ongoing, due to the presence of antipope Felix and the related schism. Nicholas V, using the tactic of reconciliation, managed to obtain the abdication of Felix V and obtain decisive recognition of his authority on behalf of the council of Basle. Shortly after the year 1449, the council finally came to a close. An able negotiator, he managed to maintain a good relationship with the European states and in particular with the Emperor: he crowned Frederick III, and he helped the Spanish to definitively push back the Saracen incursion. During his pontificate, the Roman empire of the East came to an end with the conquest of Constantinople by Mohammed II. He is buried in the Vatican Grottoes.

209 - CALLISTUS III (1455-1458). Born in Spain, Alonso Borgia was one of Alfonso V of Aragon's principal counsellors; he had followed him to Italy in 1442 when he became King of Naples. Once elected Pope, Callistus involved himself in the war against the Turks, who had conquered Constantinople. His only success was the victory in Belgrade, where he managed to push back the Turks. He was not however able to organize a true crusade. He was guilty of nepotism, especially towards his favourite nephew, making him a Cardinal. Rodrigo Borgia, his nephew, went on to become the future Alexander VI. He is buried in the Spanish Church in Rome, Saint Mary of Monserrato.

210 - PIUS II (1458-1464). Aeneas Silvius Piccolomini was born in a small town near Siena which he redesigned and remodelled as a city for the humanities, changing its name to Pienza. He was a man who cultivated humanistic interests; he was poet and wrote several books. He is known for his book of Latin poems, "*Cyntia*", and also for his autobiography in 12 books, "*Commentarii*." He became Cardinal in 1456 and gained influence during the pontificate of Nicholas V and Callistus III, who he succeeded as pontiff. He had to lofty ideals; he imagined the crusade against the Turks as the tool for the diffusion of culture for Christian civilization. In 1464, he went to Ancona with the intention of finding a fleet for an expedition against the Turks. He is buried in Saint Andrea della Valle in Rome.

211 - PAUL II (1464-1471). Born in Venice, Pietro Barbo was helped along in his ecclesiastical career by his uncle, Eugene IV, who ordained him Cardinal at a very young age. He was also a supporter of papal authority and continued efforts to realize a crusade, begun by his predecessors to stop the advancement of the Turks into the Balkans, but without success. In Rome, he lived in Saint Mark's Palace, which he had built and which later took the name Palazzo Venezia. He restarted work on Saint Peter's, entrusting it to Giuliano da Sangallo. In 1470, with a papal bull, he established that the Jubilee would be celebrated every 25 years so that every generation could have the possibility of the Jubilee pardon. He is buried in the Vatican Grottoes.

212 - SIXTUS IV (1471-1484). Born in Savona, Francesco della Rovere succeeded Paul II with the support of the Borgia, Orsini and Gonzaga cardinals. An obstinate nepotist, he maintained the Church and state with the help of his family Pietro Riario, Giuliano della Rovere and Girolamo Riario. In 1478 his nephew Girolamo involved him in the Pazzi Conspiracy against the Medici family in Florence. A debatable figure, he had absolutist pretensions and strong territorial ambitions. He was very active in politics as well as ecclesiastic areas. He declared the solemnity of the holiday of the Immaculate Conception, and instituted the holiday of Saint Joseph. He celebrated the seventh Holy year in 1475. His name is tied to the Sistine Chapel, which takes its name from him. He is buried in Saint Peter's Basilica.

213 - **INNOCENT VIII** (1484-1492). Giovanni Battista Cibo, was born in Genoa and became Pope with the support of Giuliano della Rovere. He sided with Lorenzo de Medici, making his son, who would become Pope Leo X, a Cardinal at only 13 years of age. He had a bad relationship with Ferdinand I of Naples, but later they made peace. He protected the writers and artists of the time, including Pinturicchio and Perugino. A great success during his papacy was the conquest of Granada, which was the last Turkish stronghold. During those years he condemned the slave market very strongly and gave his support to Christopher Columbus on his voyage to discover America. He is buried in Saint Peter's Basilica.

214 - **ALEXANDER VI** (1492-1503). Rodrigo Borgia was born in Spain and was the nephew of Callistus, who helped his ecclesiastical career. More than a Pope, he can be considered a Renaissance prince. Before taking religious orders, he had already had four children, the two most infamous were Caesar and Lucrezia. Many people spoke out against his moral conduct, arrogance, and against the limitless luxury in which he lived, especially Girolamo Savonarola. In 1500, he celebrated the Holy year and had three Holy Doors opened, one in the Basilica of Saint Peter's, one in Saint Paul's and another in Saint Mary Major. He is buried in the Church of Saint Mary of Monserrato, in Rome.

215 - **PIUS III** (22 September-18 October 1503). Francesco Todeschini Piccolomini of Siena, nephew of Pius II was already old and ill when he was elected Pope. He assumed the name, Pius, out of respect for his uncle. He accepted the pontificate, only after much insistence by the French and the Italian cardinals, who were rivals at the time. They wanted him as a transitional Pope after Giuliano della Rovere, who would later become Julius II, had managed to botch the election of the French Cardinal George d'Amboise. In the few days that his pontificate lasted, he demonstrated himself to be a cultivator of peace. For example, he helped save the life Caesar Borgia when his life was threatened, even though it would have better served to diminish some of the immense power that Borgia held. He is buried in the Church of Saint Andrea della Valle in Rome.

216 - **JULIUS II** (1503-1513). Born in Savona, Giuliano della Rovere was the nephew of Sixtus IV, who helped him begin a brilliant ecclesiastical career that was rich with benefits. More than a Pope, he was one of the most eminent princes of his time. He did not hesitate to lead his troops against his enemies. In 1506, Julius II began the works to construct the new Basilica of Saint Peter's, entrusting the job to Bramante. He commissioned many works from Michelangelo, including the frescoes in the Sistine chapel, while the frescoes in the Vatican rooms and loggias, he commissioned from Raphael. He called the 18th ecumenical council. He is buried in Saint Peter's Basilica.

217 - **LEO X** (1513-1521). Giovanni de Medici was born in Florence and was the son of Lorenzo the Magnificent, he became Cardinal when he was only 14 years old and he became Pope at the age of 38. He was a poet and a humanist and an incredible patron of the arts. He quickly dilapidated the patrimony left to him by his predecessors and when he did not have enough money to continue the work on Saint Peter's he began the sale of indulgences. He was unable to see the rebellious sentiments that were growing in the people. The same feelings that Martin Luther, on the other hand, was able to interpret, bringing about the Protestant schism. The Pope issued a papal bull condemning and excommunicating the Lutherans, but it arrived too late. He condemned the practice of magic and sorcery, but he was not energetic enough to repress the phenomenon. He is buried in the Roman Church of Santa Maria sopra Minerva.

218 - **ADRIAN VI** (1522-1523). Adrian of Utrecht was born in Holland and would be the last non-Italian Pope for the next 400 years. When he became Pope, he enacted a reform in the Church, worked towards the repression of Lutheranism and managed to reach an agreement among the Christian princes to unite in battle against the Turks. Attempting to find an agreement with the Lutherans, he even sent a legate to the diet of Nuremberg to declare the papacy at fault for corruption of the Church. However in Rome, his initiatives only provoked hate and criticism. When Francis I of France, descended upon Italy, the pain that the Pope felt accelerated his death. He is buried in Rome in the Church of Santa Maria dell' Anima.

219 - **CLEMENT VII** (1523-1534). Giulio de' Medici, the illegitimate son of Giuliano de Medici, was known for nepotism. He tried to use his position to win back some of his family's lost prestige in Florence, but he was extremely sober and thrifty.
His relationship with Francesco I of France cost him sorely regarding his relationship with Emperor Charles V. Romans felt the consequences in 1527, with the terrible, "Sack of Rome." His pontificate saw the rise of German Protestantism, a strong a religious divergence in Switzerland, and worst of all, the Anglican schism in England. In 1525 he called the ninth Holy year to be celebrated in Rome. He is buried in the Church of Santa Maria sopra Minerva in Rome.

220 - **PAUL III** (1534-1549). The pontificate of Roman born Alessandro Farnese, proved to be one of the most important to the Church because it marks the beginning of the Catholic Reformation. After various attempts he managed, in 1545, to call the council of Trent, where he negotiated at length to try to resolve the Protestant schism. The council closed with the reaffirmation of Catholic orthodoxy, marking the beginning of the Counter-Reformation began. He was accused of nepotism because he gave advantages to his four children, which he fathered before being ordained. A patron of the arts, he commissioned Michelangelo to do the fresco in Saint Peter's of the *"Last Judgment"*, in the Sistine Chapel. He is buried in the Basilica of Saint Peter's.

221 - **JULIUS III** (1550-1555). Born in Rome, Giovanni Maria Ciocchi del Monte, took the name of his predecessor Julius II. He, however, had a much more diplomatic and calm nature; he loved theatre, music and the arts. In politics he preferred to stay neutral between the two contenders, Emperor Charles V and Francesco II of France. He reopened the council of Trent to take back up the discussion of ecclesiastical reform. He was forced to suspend the council due to pressure from Morris of Saxony's Protestant military troops, who threatened to occupy Trento. In the meantime Protestantism continued to spread. In 1550, he celebrated tenth Holy year. He is buried in the Vatican Grottoes.

222 - **MARCELLUS II** (9 April- 1 May 1555). Marcello Cervini was born in Montepulciano and was the legate of Paul III for various diplomatic missions. He became Cardinal in 1539 and was the pontifical legate at the council of Trent and at the council of Bologna. Once elected Pope, he wanted to keep his name to demonstrate that his powerful new position would not change his lifestyle in any way. He prohibited his family from coming to Rome so that he should not fall to nepotism. He began the battle against the corruption of the Curia, asking for austerity and justice. He immediately proclaimed his neutral position between the Emperor and the King of France, asking for their help to reform the Church. He was Pope for only twenty-two days. He is buried in the Vatican Grottoes.

223 - PAUL IV (1555-1559). Giovanni Pietro Caraffa was from Naples and the family of the dukes of Montorio. He made great strides quickly in his ecclesiastical career and was elected Pope when he was nearly 80 years old. The cardinals that elected him were looking for more decisive approach to discipline in ecclesiastical life to help combat Protestantism. The cardinals realized that this energetic and inflexible man would bring about the extreme reform that was needed in the Church and that he would punish whoever needed it without giving preferences to anyone. His zeal brought him to use the tribunals of the Inquisition against Catholics and Protestants. He confined the Jewish people to the "Ghetto" in Rome. He is buried in the Church of Santa Maria sopra Minerva, in Rome.

224 - PIUS IV (1559-1565). Giovanni Angelo de Medici was born in Milan and was a milder Pope than his predecessor, overturning some of the more rigid aspect of Paul's government, including revising the more severe regulations in the Index of prohibited books. The name Pius IV is tied to the conclusion of the council of Trent, which took place in 1563, marking the triumph of the Pope. It is a memorable moment and a milestone in the history of the Church. He made his nephew, Charles Borromeo, a Cardinal. He turned out to be a good and trusted advisor and was later sainted. He was a patron of the arts; commissioning Michelangelo to transform parts of the Diocletian baths into the Church of Saint Mary of the Angels. At the end of his life, he was buried there.

225 - Saint PIUS V (1566-1572). Antonio Michele Ghisleri, once elected Pope, carried out the decrees made at the council of Trent. He worked against every form of simony and nepotism. He worked for the publication of the Roman catechism, to diffuse religious instruction and bring an end to heresy. In politics he worked towards peace between the Christian princes and resisted the Turkish advancement. His name is tied to the famous victory in Lepanto in 1571, where the Christian fleet won against the Turks. He excommunicated Queen Elizabeth of England in an attempt to bring Protestant Europe back under Rome's wing. He was made a Saint in 1712 by Clement IX. He is buried in Saint Mary Major.

226 - GREGORY XIII (1572-1585). Hugo Boncompagni was born in Bologna. He was a well-intentioned and active Pope, but with an indecisive character, that dulled the impact of his actions and ideas. While work continued on the Vatican, Gregory had the Quirinal Palace built as his summer residence, in 1573. Future popes continued to live there for periods of time, until 1870. In the year 1575, Gregory celebrated the 11th Holy Year. His name is tied to the famous Gregorian calendar reform, which was based on changing the official calendar year to match the astronomical calendar year, from October 5th the date became October 15th, during the year 1582. Ten days of history disappeared in the blink of an eye. He is buried in Saint Peter's Basilica.

227 - SIXTUS V (1585 1590). Felice Peretti was born of humble origins (in Grottammare). Helped by his strength of character and his ingenious and noble soul, he was elected as Pope by unanimous vote. Pope Sixtus, with his rigour, was able to give peace of mind and security back to the Roman citizens, even if he at times he succeeded in doing so with impious activities; in fact, he condemned many people to the death. He was an illuminated patron of the arts: Rome was reborn under his reign of with his multiple public works. In foreign policy he supported the unlucky reign of Philip II of Spain, when in 1588, "*the invincible Armada*" was defeated in a naval battle against the fleet of Elizabeth of England. He is buried in Saint Mary Major.

228 - **URBAN VII** (15-27 September 1590). Giambattista Castagna was born in Rome to a family with origins in Genoa. He was the papal nuncio in Spain, in the city of Venice and in Poland. He was the legate at the council of France for Pius IV. He made Gregory XIII, a Cardinal in the year 1583 and he always worked diligently with love of justice and charity. He was Pope for only 13 days because he suddenly died from malaria. From the moment he was elected, however, he presented himself as a faithful follower of the trident decrees, and he worked to help needy children. He left all of his belongings to charity and he is buried in the Church of Santa Maria sopra Minerva.

229 - **GREGORY XIV** (1590-1591). Niccolò Spondrati had a degree in law from Pavia, then he answered the calling of the ecclesiastical life and became the Bishop of Cremona and in 1583 he was made Cardinal. He was a mild-tempered man with stronger leanings towards mysticism and pastoral action, than towards politics. He allowed his nephews and others to act as his political advisors, but they revealed themselves to be incapable. They advised him to trust Philip II, which put him in contrast with Henry IV, who he excommunicated. He had a great love for the people and did much to try and alleviate their suffering during the plague. He is buried in Saint Peter's Basilica.

230 - **INNOCENT IX** (29 October-30 December 1591). Giovanni Antonio Facchinetti was born in Bologna of modest origins and demonstrated himself to be a man of great culture and to have a good understanding of ecclesiastical affairs. He was much loved by the Roman people when he was elected Pope and his death, which happened only two months later, was felt deeply in the city. His first act of office was to furnish the city with grain and bring an end to banditry and the fighting between internal factions. He had also begun to balance the Vatican finances. He is buried in the Vatican Grottoes.

231 - **CLEMENT VIII** (1592-1605). Ippolito Aldobrandini was born in Florence, but his papal election was supported by the votes of the Spanish cardinals. He sustained the autonomy of the Church regarding Spain's anti-French policy, cancelled the excommunication of Henry IV and worked towards bringing peace to France, which was disrupted by religious wars. In Italy, he consolidated the Catholic reform and carried out the rulings of the council of Trent. He conceded his esteem to valiant men, including Roberto Bellarmino, who was later made a Saint and to whom he entrusted the tribunal of the Inquisition. He also carried out some exemplary punishments, such as Beatrice Cenci and Giordano Bruno, whom he had burned at the stake. In 1600 he celebrated the Holy year. He is buried in Saint Mary Major.

232 - **LEO XI** (1-27 April 1605). Born in Florence, Alessandro Ottaviano de Medici, nephew of Leo X and the Archbishop of Florence, was elected to avoid the probable election of the Spanish Cardinal. The people approved his election, used to the natural generosity of the Medici's, made even more so considering that King Henry IV of France was married to Maria de Medici. Leo made it immediately clear to Philip II, that even though he had family bonds, he would remain impartial. Leo XI was Pope for only 27 days and died due to a sickness he got on the day that Lateran was attacked. He was buried in Saint Peter's and his tomb is adorned with a monument by Algardi.

233 - PAUL V (1605-1621). Born in Rome, Camillo Borghese was a jurist and a well-known diplomat. Among the important events that happened during his pontificate was the clamorous contrast with the Republic of Venice, brought about by his desire to defend the interests of the Church. The incident ended with the excommunication of the Senate and the Venetian Doges in 1606. Paul V also ended the theological disputes between the Dominicans and the Jesuits. He also approved the condemnation of that Copernican system, even though he had a positive attitude towards astronomy. He did much to care for the urban aspects of Rome: he is responsible for many works including having Maderno finish the façade of Saint Peter's and the splendid apse of Saint Mary Major, which is also the location of his tomb.

234 - GREGORY XV (1621-1623). Alessandro Ludovisi was born in Bologna. In just two years he was able to make noteworthy changes, aided by his nephew Ludwig. He wrote a new constitution, fixing new rules for the conclave, reinstating the importance of secrecy, so that future conclaves were less pressured by external political influences. He began the congregation, Propaganda Fide, and regularly organized missions. He canonized Saint Theresa and Saint Philip Neri. He supported the Catholic restoration of Ferdinand II of Austria and supported Louis XIII in his actions against the French Huguenots. He is buried in Rome in the Church of Saint Ignatius.

235 - URBAN VIII (1623-1644). Born in Florence, Maffeo Barberini was a brilliant and well-educated man. He was a patron of the arts and kept several artists under his protection including Bernini, Carlo Maderno, as well as writers and poets of the time. In Rome, he is responsible for building the Barberini Palace and for the papal villa in Castel Gandolfo. He worked towards the systematic urbanization of Rome, and left baroque architectural influences in the city. He had the Pantheon restored, but unfortunately he had the bronzes taken off the cupola and used on the winding columns of the baldachin in Saint Peter's. He was called the "*gabella Pope*" for the sharp rise in taxes that was required to sustained his works. In 1625 he celebrated the 13th Holy year. He is buried in Saint Peter's.

236 - INNOCENT X (1644-1655). Born in Rome, Giambattista Pamfili was elected September 15, 1644. In 1648 with the peace of Westphalia, the Pope saw the end of the Thirty Year War and the victory of the Protestants. In 1649, he supported the Venetians in the war against the Turks. Pope Innocent contributed to the architectural and artistic betterment of Rome. He is given credit for restructuring Piazza Navona and for building Saint Agnes Church, commissioning Borromini to do the work. He is also responsible for the Bernini Fountains facing the square in Villa Pamphili Park. He condemned Jansenism and was very sensitive towards the needs of the powerless. In 1650 he celebrated the 14th Holy year. He is buried in the Church of Saint Agnes in Rome.

237 - ALEXANDER VII (1655-1667). Born in Siena, Fabio Chigi refused to sign the protocols of the peace treaty of Westphalia from 1648. He considered the measures unfair, because they sanctioned the Christian schism between Protestants and Catholics and imposed terrible conditions on the Catholics. He was unyielding with the Jansenists and wrote many things against them. He had bitter conflicts with French King Louis XIV and with Cardinal Mazzarino, who had initially backed his election. Alexander was a man of culture and a lover of the arts; various public works are credited to him. He is known and above all for the Piazza of Saint Peter's by Bernini. He is buried in Saint Peter's.

238 - **CLEMENT IX** (1667-1669). Born in Pistoia, Giulio Rospigliosi, rose to the papal throne with the help of French faction cardinals. He worked towards the peace at Aquisgrana in 1668 between the Louis XIV and Spain, hoping to be able to lead a crusade against the Turks, a goal he was never able to reach. When Candia (Crete) fell into Turkish hands, in 1669, he was very saddened by the loss. He was a philosopher, a scientist and a poet. He commissioned John Lorenzo Bernini to sculpt many statues that adorn the colonnade of Saint Peter's. He was benevolent towards the Jewish people and generous with the poor. He was not guilty of nepotism, even if he did elect his nephew, Giacomo Rospigliosi, as Cardinal. He is buried in Saint Mary Major.

239 - **CLEMENT X** (1670-1676). Emilio Bonaventura Altieri, was Roman born and elected Pope when was already in his eighties. For this reason he delegated nearly all of his power to Cardinal Paluzzo Paluzzi, to whom he gave his family name Alteri and left all his worldly goods. Unfortunately the Cardinal was very unpopular and this reflected negatively on the Pope, who was actually a mild and charitable man. He sorely felt the fall of Candia and he backed the Catholic King of Poland, John Sobieskj, to help organize allies against the Muslims. With the spirit of the crusade, the popes celebrated a Jubilee in 1675 that was characterized by great festivities. Even Queen Cristina of Sweden was in Rome that year. He is buried in Saint Peter's Basilica.

240 - **Blessed INNOCENT XI** (1676-1689). Born in Como, Benedetto Odescalchi was decisively against nepotism and imposed a regime of harsh austerity on the pontifical courts. Innocent was untiring in sustaining John Sobieskj of Poland, who liberated Vienna in 1685 during the siege of the Turks. This defeat marked the beginning of the fall of Muslim domination in the Balkans. He had strong differences with the French King Louis XIV, who wanted power in affairs of the clergy and expected the rights of asylum and immunity for his ambassadors in Rome. He prohibited lending with usury, gambling, and stigmatized every lapse. He also gave a great input to the teaching of catechism. He is buried in Saint Peter's Basilica.

241 - **ALEXANDER VIII** (1689-1691). Pietro Vito Ottoboni was born in Venice and was nominated by Urban VIII, of the *Sacra Rota,* as Cardinal and then became Bishop of Brescia in 1654. Ten years later, in Rome, he gained influence with Innocent XI. He was elected Pope in 1689, while all of Europe was at war. He reconciled with King Louis XIV, reaching a semi-compromise regarding the "*Galician Liberties,*" which he later annulled unilaterally. He helped the Venetians in the battle against the Turks. With his personal funds, he bought Cristina of Sweden's library and donated it to the Vatican library. He reduced taxes and made great concessions to farmers, leaving them free to sell their grain. He is buried in Saint Peter's Basilica.

242 - **INNOCENT XII** (1691-1700). Antonio Pignatelli was born in Puglia and had a mild character, he was a well-educated and virtuous Pope. His name is tied to the anti-nepotism reform, with a papal bull in 1692, he officially condemned nepotism. Later he made provisions to stop the sale of bureaucratic positions and ecclesiastical titles. He earned the nickname "*father of the needy*" because of the numerous efforts he made in favour of the poor. He finally reached a diplomatic solution to resolve the conflicts with Louis XIV and get him to renounce the "*Galician Liberties.*" In exchange, the Pope recognized the bishops that had been nominated by the King. In 1700, he celebrated the Holy year, but did not see itd end, because he died in September of that year. He is buried in Saint Peter's Basilica.

243 - **CLEMENT XI** (1700-1721). Giovanni Francesco Albani was born in Urbino and was elected almost immediately after the death of his predecessor, because a pontiff was needed to conclude the Holy year. He was elected on November 23, 1700. A man of culture and a lover of the arts, he was elected Pope by vote of the Spanish cardinals. However, he maintained an ambiguous position during the Spanish war of secession, first backing Phillip V of Spain, then later Charles VI of Austria. His pontificate was marked by the resurgence of the Jansenist theories. He was unyieldimg in his fight against them; in fact, in 1713 he condemned them as heretics, issuing the papal bull "*Unigenitus*." He is buried under the choir floor in Saint Peter's Basilica.

244 - **INNOCENT XIII** (1721-1724). Born in Rome, Michelangelo de Conti, a relative of the dukes of Poli, was a wise man, who found himself involved in the complex political clashes taking place throughout Europe with Phillip V's war against Spain. Slowly, the political and religious controversies subsided and in 1723, Innocent signed a compromise with Spain to reform the nation according to the spirit of the council of Trent. He conferred the reign of Naples on Emperor Charles VI. He had some divergences of opinion with King John of Portugal who wanted the privilege of the *placet* on the nomination of the pontifical nuncio in his kingdom. He is buried in the Vatican Grottoes.

245 - **BENEDICT XIII** (1724-1730). Pietro Francesco Orsini belonged to a noble Roman family which already had ties to the pontificate. He served as the Bishop of Benevento for many years, a diocese that he tried to maintain, even as Pope.
Benedict was an ascetic and pious man who had no idea how to govern, so he delegated many matters of government to Nicholas Coscia, who revealed himself to be an intriguing and undeserving individual. The Pope occupied himself nearly exclusively to spiritual matters. In 1725 he celebrated the Holy year and inaugurated the imposing stairway of Trinità dei Monti, at the Spanish steps. He is buried in the Church of Santa Maria sopra Minerva.

246 - **CLEMENT XII** (1730-1740). Born in Florence, Lorenzo Corsini, was elected Pope and was very severe with Cardinal Coscia, who had abused the trust of Benedict XIII. He also excommunicated Masons in 1738; Masonry had been imported from England just a few years earlier and had spread through Rome, Naples and Tuscany. Anti-curial politics began in Naples with Bernardo Tanucci and would trouble the pontificate for the next 50 years. Overall, Clement was a great administrator and is remembered for providing better public buildings inside and outside Rome. He is remembered for the fountain of Trevy in Rome, by architect Salvi. He is buried in Lateran.

247 - **BENEDICT XIV** (1740-1758). Prospero Lorenzo Lambertini was born in Bologna, and when he became Pope he continued to behave as he always had. He was interested in the real problems of the people and went to various neighbourhoods throughout the city to visit them and he made many gestures of mercy. He abolished the Inquisition which was still functioning in Tuscany. He reaffirmed the condemnation of Masonry. In politics, he was guided by a reconciliatory spirit, stipulating treaties with Portugal, Naples, Sardinia and Spain. He exchanged letters with Voltaire, who praised the doctrines and the virtues of this Pope. In 1750, he celebrated the 18th Jubilee and pilgrims came to Rome from every part of the world to celebrate. He is buried in Saint Peter's Basilica.

248 - **CLEMENT XIII** (1758-1769). Carlo Rezzonico was born in Venice. Once elected Pope, he did not share the tolerant attitudes and personality of his predecessor in religious and cultural matters. He fought against the diffusion of Illuminist theories and contrasted the principles of Illuminist despotism. He had the works of Rousseau and the "*Encyclopedie*," prohibited in the Index. Clement, always defended the Jesuits and ignored the request of major states to suppress the order. His refusal cost him their support and in some cases disrupted relations with Catholic states. He is buried in Saint Peter's.

249 - **CLEMENT XIV** (1769-1774). Giovanni Vincenzo Ganganelli was elected on compromise, after three months without a Pope. He soon issued the decree, for which he had obtained the pontifical throne, the disbanding of the Jesuits, who were later regrouped by Pius VII in 1814. The Bourbon courts were satisfied with this decision and gave the Sainted Seat back its dominion over Avignon and Benevento. He created the Clement Museum in the Vatican. He was a charitable soul and he loved the simple life, but his pontificate was surrounded by untrustworthy and rebellious priests. He died in September 1774 after having called the Jubilee for the year 1775. He is buried in the Roman Church Santissimi Apostoli.

250 - **PIUS VI** (1775-1799). He was born in Cesena. Giovanni Angelico Braschi, as soon as he was elected Pope, he opened the Holy year that had been called by his predecessor. He tried to oppose the reforms that had taken place, to the disadvantage of the Church, in Germany, Russia, Naples and Austria. The revolution in France and the affirmation of Napoleon weighed heavily on the pontiff and had long-lasting consequences. With the treaty of Tolentino, Pius VI had to renounce Avignon and the legate of Bologna, Ferrara, and all of Romagna. In 1798, after the occupation of the Church state, the Roman Republic was proclaimed, ending the temporal power of the Church. Pius VI was imprisoned and he died in exile in the citadel of Valence. He is buried in Saint Peter's.

251 - **PIUS VII** (1800-1823). Barnaba Chiaramonti was elected Pope after a long and difficult conclave held in Venice. Pious VII was the only European sovereign to hold out against the incredible power of Napoleon. In July of 1801 he stipulated a compromise with Napoleon which regulated relations between the Church and state. In 1804, he crowned Napoleon Emperor in the Cathedral of Notre Dame in Paris, but in the following years the relationship deteriorated as all of the pontifical states were slowly absorbed by Napoleon. The Pope finally excommunicated him. The Emperor responded by ordering the arrest of Pius VII, keeping him prisoner until 1813. The next year, when the Pope returned to Rome, he reinstated the Jesuits. He is buried in Saint Peter's.

252 - **LEO XII** (182 3-1829). Annibale della Genga, in the encyclical that he wrote right after being elected, "*Ubi Primum*," revealed himself and his policies to be extremely conservative. He condemned sects and secret societies and delegated Cardinal Rivarola to repress the Carbonarist movements in Romagna. He was against any sort of liberal idea and took laymen out of administrative roles. In contrast, he took the writings of Galileo off of the Index of forbidden books. Leo was a good man and he helped the poor. He also worked for the reconstruction of the Basilica of Saint Paul's and to restore the Vatican palaces where he resided. In 1825 he celebrated the 20th Jubilee, held in Rome with more than 500,000 pilgrims in attendance. He is buried in Saint Peter's.

253 - **PIUS VIII** (1829-1830). Francesco Xaverio Castiglioni, was a Pope with a mild character and was well-liked in both France and Austria, who were pleased not have a pontiff "zealot" like his predecessor. He demonstrated a moderate liking for liberal groups and was convinced that it was better to adopt a persuasive and reconciliatory attitude. In an encyclical, he denounced the decay of religion and of moral and social order cause by the developments in social criticism and ideologies of secret societies. He fought against these groups, but not excessively. He began the Vatican state Postal Service and strengthened the missions throughout the world; he is buried in Saint Peter's.

254 - **GREGORY XVI** (1831-1846). Born in Belluno, Bartolomeo Alberto Cappellari was a monk of the order of Calmaldoli and had chosen the religious name Mauro. He immediately became famous as a reactionary Pope. In some encyclicals his attitude is explicit and he shows himself sensitive only to the interests of the princes and powerful. Regarding the constitutional and revolutionary movements, in central Italy during 1831, he asked for help from Austria and for this he was judged very severely. He was against freedom of the press; he condemned the liberal Catholicism of Lamennais. He increased the number of archaeological digs in the forum and the catacombs; he favoured philosophical studies of Abbot Anthony Rosmini. He is buried in Saint Peter's.

255 - **Blessed PIUS IX** (1846-1878). Giovanni Maria Mastai-Ferretti demonstrated himself to be a moderate Pope and a friend of the liberals. In 1848, when the Roman Republic was proclaimed, he had to flee to Gaeta and later assumed a conservative stance, to defend papal power. When Italy was reunified and the reign of Italy was proclaimed in 1870, Pius IX had to accept the end of the temporal reign of papal power. This was the beginning of the "Roman question." He closed himself in the Vatican palaces and did not leave them ever again, not even during the Holy year which was celebrated in 1875. He was declared Blessed on September 3, 2000 during the Jubilee by Pope John Paul II.

256 - **LEO XIII** (187 8-1903). Born in Spoleto, Gioacchino Pecci was elected Pope in a conclave that lasted only 36 hours. He vindicated the possession of Rome without contesting the unity of Italy. He supported the political policy in Bismarck, and worked as a negotiator between France and Germany, but his real intention was always to bring the Church back to its ancient grandness. With the encyclical "*Rerum Novarum*," in 1891, he outlined the position of the Church regarding social questions. He took a hard-line with the Italian state, prohibiting Catholics from participating in political life. During the Holy year of 1900, the façade and the cupola of Saint Peter's were lit with "electric lights" for the first time. He is buried in Lateran.

257 - **Saint**. **PIUS X** (1903-1914). Born in Riese, Giuseppe Sarto asked for the cooperation of the Secretary of State Merry del Valle to bring out a series of betterments in religious life: giving value to communion, and reforming the Roman Breviary. He took care with instruction in the catechism, publishing the famous "*Catechisms*", and began the codification of canonical law; he organized the curia and founded the Bible Institute. In his relations with the Italian state and the Roman question, he was unyielding; he was equally firm about the introduction of innovative ideas in theological studies. He tried in every way possible to stop World War I. He was canonized in 1954 by Pius XII. He is buried in Saint Peter's Basilica.

258 - **BENEDICT XV** (1914-1922). Giacomo della Chiesa was born in Genoa and followed the policies of Leo XIII. He restored prestige and authority to the pontificate and was a significant force in international politics, which was notable because of the World War I. During the conflicts, he gave an enormous amount of help to prisoners and to the countries that were hardest hit and he never tired of speaking at peace summits with heads of state. In those years the Church re-established diplomatic relations with Europe and the first steps were taken towards reconciliation between the Italian state and the Roman question. He diffused the codex of canonical law, and gave precise directives to the heads of missions. He is buried in the Vatican Grottoes.

259 - **PIUS XI** (1922-1939). Achille Ratti was very open towards the Italian state and towards resolving the Roman question. This openness was welcomed by the government, which collaborated with the Vatican during the Holy year of 1925, offering transport and traffic control. Preparations for the event were laid out in the Lateran pacts, signed in Lateran, 1929. The Pact decided that the state of Vatican City and its territories were independent from the Italian state. In 1931, the Pope inaugurated the most important radio transmitter in the world, together with Guglielmo Marconi. In 1933 he called the first "extraordinary Jubilee of the Redemption" for the 19th centennial of the death and resurrection of Jesus. He is buried in the Vatican Grottoes.

260 - **PIUS XII** (1939-1958). Eugenio Pacelli was born in Rome and was elected Pope by unanimous vote. He immediately tried to stop the war, which in 1939 was looming on the horizon. He preached of peace, in vain, and then he began to organize a vast network providing assistance, humanitarian aid and information. At the end of the conflicts, Pius XII became more rigid and declared himself against communist ideology. In 1950, he celebrated the 24th Jubilee and in that year he proclaimed the dogma of the Assumption of the Virgin Mary and he began the archaeological digs under the confessional of Saint Peter's, in which his sepulchre was brought to light. He is buried in the Vatican Grottoes.

261 - **Saint JOHN XXIII** (1958-1963). Angelo Giuseppe Roncalli will always be remembered as the "*good Pope*". Just three months after his election, he called the second ecumenical Vatican council on October 11, 1962. The ecumenical council marked the beginnings of a fundamental renewal in the Catholic Church. His pastoral visits throughout Rome are famous, as well the spirit of welcome and lovingness that distinguished him as a man and as a Pope. Beatified on 3 September, during the 2000 Jubilee, by Pope John Paul II, he was officially sanctified on 27 April 2014 together with Pope John Paul II. He is buried in Saint Peter's basilica.

262 - **PAUL VI** (1963-1978). Giovanni Battista Montini followed in the footsteps of his predecessors in welcoming innovative new programs. Right after his election, he called the second Vatican ecumenical council, opening a new relationship with all of the other Christian Churches and monotheistic religions. He was however opposed to certain behaviours emerging in the modern Catholic and lay world. In the encyclical, "*Umanae Vitae*," he spoke out against birth control. Paul VI celebrated the Jubilee in 1975: more than 1.300.000.000 people watched the opening of the Holy Door of the Basilica of Saint Peter's with world-vision. He is buried in the Vatican Grottoes.

263 - **JOHN PAUL I** (26 August-28 September 1978). Albino Luciani was born in the province of Belluno and was from a modest family. He was ordained as a priest in 1935. He graduated with a degree in theology in Rome and was called by Paul VI to become a Cardinal and to guide the diocese of Venice. When he was elected Pope he decided to take a double name, something that had never happened before, to indicate his pontificate's continuity with the last two pontificates. He died of a heart attack only 33 days after the beginning at his pontificate without ever having time to present his pastoral program. He was called the "smiling Pope," because he was good humoured, humane, down to earth and beyond the temptations of temporal power. He is buried in the Vatican Grottoes.

264 - **Saint JOHN PAUL II** (16 October 1978-2 April 2005). Born in Wadowice, in Poland on May 18, 1920 with the name Karol Wojtyla, he was the first Polish pontiff and the first non-Italian Pope after 455 years; the last had been the Dutch Adrian VI. He had the longest running pontificate in the history of the Church, after Pius IX. In 1946 he graduated with a degree in theology, from the University of Krakow, and was ordained as priest in the same year. He began a lively pastoral activity above all with young people and workers. When he was just 38 years old he was nominated as an auxiliary Bishop to Krakow and he became Archbishop after having actively participated in the second Vatican council in 1967. In the

same year he was nominated Cardinal by Paul VI. Elected Pope on October 16, 1978 he guided the Church with authority, love and dedication. John Paul II gave a strong input and great importance to ecumenical dialogue and he worked towards the unity of all Christians. In 1979 he went to Turkey to meet the Orthodox Patriarch of Constantinople. In 1986, he made a gesture of reconciliation, being the first Pope to ever go to the synagogue in Rome, where he prayed together with the Jewish people, defining them "*big brothers*." In 1989 he received the president of the Soviet Union, Mikhail Gorbachev, at the Vatican. The "*missionary*" Pope, John Paul II travelled 1,247,000 kilometres in the 26 years of his pontificate making 104 trips outside Italy and visiting 131 countries on all of the continents. His Eastern policy *Ostpolitik*, of the 1980s contributed to the fall of communism in Eastern Europe and the ex-Soviet Union, symbolically represented by fall of the Berlin Wall in 1989. In 1993, during his trip to Sicily, he took a hard stand against the Mafia. He frequently called attention to Western capitalist policies asking for less frenetic consumerism and a more tangible generosity regarding the Third World countries and the Fourth World, asking that the rich in industrialized countries cancel the debts of those states. He constantly implored peace to the governments of all countries, belligerent and non, so he can also be defined as the "*Pope of peace*." He was the Bishop of Rome in the true sense of the word and he regularly visited the churches in the city. In May 1981, he was the victim of a terrible assault in Saint Peter's Square by the Turkish man Ali Agca. The event shocked the world, which followed the event with its breath held tight as John Paul II struggled between life and death, confronting his pain with courage and Christian spirit. Pope Wojtyla proclaimed 488 Saints (including Padre Pio) and declared 1345 Blessed (including Mother Teresa of Calcutta and John XXIII), many more nominations than his predecessors had ever made. He wrote 14 encyclical letters, many of which talk about principals of the faith and the position of the Church regarding various arguments such as social justice and the defence of life and Christian ethics. In 1983 he celebrated the extraordinary Holy year of the Redemption. With the letter, "*Tertio millenio adveniente*," John Paul II began preparations for the grand Jubilee to celebrate the year 2000. During that Jubilee year he solemnly pronounced the "*mea culpa*" in Saint Peter's for errors committed by the Church during the course of the centuries. During the war against Iraq, he defended peace and the United Nations as the supreme and legitimate representation of the peoples of the world. His aging was somewhat heroic; the more his body became heavy with age the stronger his impulse grew to guide the Church.
John Paul II died during the evening of April 2, 2005. Three million faithful followers watched, especially the "*papa boys*," and came from all over the world for the occasion of his funeral. They testified of their pain, as well as of their adoration and gratitude to this much loved and adored Pope, so much that an emotional collective cry rose up: "*Saint Immediately!*" After his beatification ceremony on 1 May 2011, his body was moved from the Vatican Grottoes, where it was laid to rest in 2005, to the Chapel of St. Sebastian inside St. Peter's Basilica. John Paul II was canonized by Pope Francis on 27 April 2014 together with Pope John XXIII.

265 - BENEDICT XVI (April 19, 2005-February 28, 2013, by abdication). Joseph Ratzinger was born on April 16, 1927 in Marktl am Inn, in the diocese of Passau in Germany. He is descended from an old, modest southern Bavarian family. During his adolescence he lived through the horrors of World War II and at the age of only sixteen he was called up for duty in the auxiliary anti-aircraft service. In the difficult years that followed the war, he took up the study of Philosophy at the University of Munich, and continued with it at the School of Philosophy and Theology of Freising. On June 29, 1951, he was ordained as priest and in 1953 earned his doctorate in Theology at the University of Munich.

He subsequently became a university professor of Theology, working at some of the most prestigious universities in Germany. Since 1962, he has gained an international reputation by participating as a theological consultant at the Vatican II Council. Appointed, by Paul VI, Archbishop of Munich and Freising (March 25, 1977), and later, Cardinal-Priest of Santa Maria Consolatrice al Tiburtino (June 27, 1977), he was then called to the Vatican by John Paul II to hold the important role of Prefect of the Congregation for the Doctrine of the Faith (November 25, 1981). He was the President of the Pontifical Biblical Commission and of the International Theological Commission (1981), as well as the President of the Commission for the Catechism Preparation of the Catholic Church (1986-1992).

On April 5, 1993, he became Cardinal-Bishop, was elected Vice-Dean of the College of Cardinals (since 1998) and afterwards as Dean of the Sacred College (2002). At the opening of the Conclave, Ratzinger was already considered a candidate, considered an element of continuity, testimony and as a protagonist during the past decades of the Church. On April 19, 2005, after just twenty-four hours of Conclave, Joseph Ratzinger was elected as Pope Benedict XVI, at the age of 78. One hundred thousand faithful gathered in Saint Peter's Square after his election was announced. Benedict defined himself as "a simple and humble worker in the vineyard of the Lord". During his pontificate he has written three Encyclicals. The first, "Deus Caritas est", in 2006, deals with the loving relationship between a man and a woman. The second, "Spe Salvi", published in 2007, presents the positivity of hope, by virtue of which we can face our present. With the third encyclical, "Caritas in Veritate", 2009, Benedict XVI states he is in favour of development on a human level, implying new ways of life. In May 2011, the previous Pope was proclaimed Blessed Pope John Paul II, just six years after his death. The Pope, during his eight years of pontificate, has noted with dismay a "Church with a disfigured, scarred, torn face, due to the errors of its children, from the simple faithful to the bishops and cardinals". He has also fought, with courage and determination, for the recognition of religious freedom in the world.

In his final years of pontificate he has condemned religious hypocrisy, behaviour just for appearance sake and attitudes that seek applause and approval. He has also railed against those who expose the Church "to mockery and derision by the people". And at the Angelus of condemnation on February 17, facing a massive crowd, he uttered harsh words against "the false images of man that, at every moment, threaten our conscience, in the guise of suitable, effective and even good proposals, placing everyone at a crossroads: do we want to follow our ego or God".

On 11 February 2013, during the Consistory, Benedict XVI announced his historic and moving resignation: his abdication from "the ministry of the Bishop of Rome, successor of St. Peter, entrusted to me by the hand of the Cardinals April 19, 2005"; the reason being: "After having repeatedly examined my conscience before God, I have come to the certainty that my strengths, due to an advanced age, are no longer suited to an adequate exercise of the Petrine ministry. I am well aware that this ministry, due to its essential spiritual nature, must be carried out not only with words and deeds, but no less with prayer and suffering. However, in today's world, subject to so many rapid changes and shaken by questions of deep relevance for the life of faith, in order to govern the boat of Saint Peter and proclaim the Gospel, both strength of mind and body are necessary, strength which in the last few months, has deteriorated in me to the extent that I have had to recognise my incapacity to adequately fulfil the ministry entrusted to me".

On 28 February 2013, Benedict XVI left the Vatican by helicopter and moved temporarily into the papal summer residence of Castel Gandolfo. Here, from the balcony of the papal palace he said goodbye to the emotional, faithful crowd as a "pilgrim": "Thank you for your love, good night". From 8pm of the same day he took the title of Pope Emeritus. After about two months he will settle into his residence in the small monastery of Mater Ecclesiae in the Vatican.

266 - **FRANCIS** (13 March 2013). Jorge Mario Bergoglio was born in Buenos Aires on 17 December 1936 and since 13 March 2013 has been the 266th Bishop of Rome and Pope of the Catholic Church.

The Pope is Argentinian, but of Italian origin, specifically Piedmont; he is the first of five children of Mario, an accountant, and Regina Maria Sivori. Bergoglio is the first pope who is a member of the congregation of the Society of Jesus and the first from the American continent. Another new aspect is that he is the first Pope, after eleven centuries, to adopt a name that has never been used before by a predecessor. Described as a simple and shy boy, during his youth he studied and graduated as a Consultant Chemist. He took up a short period of employment. His religious turning point was at age 22: Jorge moved into the seminary in Villa Devoto to pursue a priestly life. On 11 March 1958 he began his novitiate in the Society of Jesus, spending a period in Chile and returning to Buenos Aires for a degree in Philosophy in 1960. In 1964 he taught Literature and Psychology in the Colegio de la Inmaculada in Santa Fe and in 1966 in the Colegio del Salvador in Buenos Aires. From 1967 to 1970 he studied Theology at the Philosophical and Theological Faculty of San Miguel, where he graduated. On 13 December 1969 he was ordained a priest. After several teaching experiences and his appointment as Provincial Superior of Argentina (1973 to 1979) he became rector of the Faculty of Theology and Philosophy at San Miguel. These were very difficult years for Argentina, which was stifled by a merciless dictatorship. It was difficult also for the Church, that felt a duty to support the oppressed classes, but that sometimes found itself being subjected to the power and blackmail of the military. In 1979 he took part in the summit of the Latin American Episcopal Conference in Puebla. On 20 May 1992 Blessed Pope John Paul II appointed him Titular Bishop of Auca and Auxiliary Bishop of Buenos Aires. On 27 June of the same year he received priestly ordination in the Cathedral of Buenos Aires. On 28 February 1998 he was appointed Archbishop of Buenos Aires. Since the beginning of his episcopal ministry, he has chosen a simple and austere lifestyle. Since 1946, he has been a fan of a famous Argentinian football club, San Lorenzo; giving up the benefits granted by his top ecclesiastical office, he frequently uses public transport, he lives in a modest apartment where he prepares dinner alone. "My people are poor", he has often said, "and I'm one of them." He has always advised his priests to show mercy, apostolic courage and doors open to everyone. He is the author of the books: "Meditaciones para religiosos" in 1982, "Reflexiones sobre la vida apostólica" in 1986 and "Reflexiones de esperanza" in 1992. He is Ordinary for the Faithful of the Eastern Rite living in Argentina. On 21 February 2001 Blessed John Paul II ordained him cardinal of the title of St. Robert Bellarmine. In the 2005 conclave, in which Pope Benedict XVI was elected, Bergoglio was the cardinal with the most votes after Ratzinger. From 2005 to 2011, he was head of the Argentine Episcopal Conference. He is also advisor of the Pontifical Commission for Latin America, Chancellor of the Catholic University of Argentina, President of the Episcopal Commission for the Pontifical Catholic University of Argentina, a member of the Congregation for Divine Worship and the Discipline of the Sacraments, a member of the Congregation for the Clergy, a member of the Congregation for Institutes of Consecrated Life and Societies of Apostolic Life, a member of the Executive Committee of the Pontifical Council for the Family and a member of the Post Synodal Apostolic Exhortation. On 22 February 2013 Pope Benedict XVI appointed Cardinal Bergoglio a member of the Pontifical Commission for Latin America. On 11 February 2013 Benedict XVI announces his historic resignation from the papacy. During the Conclave of the Cardinals, gathered at the Sistine Chapel for the election of the new Pope, on 13 March 2013, at the fifth count, Jorge Mario Bergoglio was elected Pope taking on the name Francis in honour of Saint Francis of Assisi. In his first speech in the role of the Bishop of Rome and Pope of the Catholic Church, overlooking St. Peter's Square overflowing with the faithful and, after having affectionately greeted the crowd with a friendly and simple "good evening", he asked us to pray for Pope Emeritus Benedict XVI, reciting together with all the faithful the Lord's Prayer, the Hail Mary and Glory Be to the Father. With a gesture of great compassion he then asked the faithful to also pray for him. Peter's 266th successor, he presents himself as a humble shepherd, capable of looking at a universal Church that spreads "the announcement of God's love and mercy" everywhere, bringing his style as an energetic and capable Bishop and preacher to the Vatican. A few days after his election, the historic encounter of the two Popes: for the first time two Popes – Pope Francis and Pope Emeritus Joseph Ratzinger prayed together in the pontifical palace of Castel Gandolfo. As soon as he was raised to the papal throne, Pope Francis started a series of institutional and economic reforms of the Curia, of the IOR (Istituto per le Opere di Religione - Institute for the Works of Religion - , commonly known as the Vatican's Bank) and of the Vatican's penal code with the aim to reorganize the Holy See. From his very first steps, Pope Bergoglio has proven to be very innovative, in refusing to live in the apostolic palace and choosing instead to reside in the Domus Santa Marta; in wearing a silver cross (instead of gold), in moving around in ordinary cars and if possible, refusing the body guard, and in dressing with sobriety.

Like John Paul II, he interprets the pastoral mission by setting off on a number of apostolic visits during which he never fails to preach peace, solidarity and support to the weaker. On various occasions he stigmatizes the inadequacy of the more advanced countries in receiving migrants and in handling this tragic and epochal phenomenon. He tries to be close to people by visiting them in hospitals, in jails, in mental homes and orphanages. He has words of comfort or an embrace for everyone. If asked, he does not hesitate to write or telephone personally. His words, suited to the modern world, are able to reach people's hearts and bring the faithful closer to a Catholic Church which is open to contemporary society.

The cardinals gathered in the Sistine Chapel for the Conclave that elected Pope Francis.

© Servizio Fotografico de "L' Osservatore Romano"

© Servizio Fotografico de "L'Osservatore Romano"

Pope Francis

CHRONOLOGICAL LIST OF THE POPES

1 - St. PETER (67)
2 - (St.) LINUS (67-76)
3 - (St.) ANACLETUS (Ist cen.)
4 - St. CLEMENT I (88-97)
5 - St. EVARISTUS (97-105)
6 - St. ALEXANDER I (105-115)
7 - (St.) SIXTUS I (115-125)
8 - (St.) TELESPHORUS (125-136)
9 - (St.) HYGINUS (136-140)
10 - St. PIUS I (140-155)
11 - (St.) ANICETUS (155-166)
12 - (St.) SOTER (166-175)
13 - St. ELEUTHERIUS (175-189)
14 - St. VICTOR I (189-199)
15 - St. ZEPHYRINUS (199-217)
16 - St. CALLISTUS I (217-22)
17 - St. URBAN I (222-30)
18 - St. PONTIAN (230-35)
19 - St. ANTERUS (235-36)
20 - St. FABIAN (236-50)
21 - St. CORNELIUS (251-53)
22 - (St.) LUCIUS (253-54)
23 - St. STEPHEN I (254-257)
24 - St. SIXTUS II (257-258)
25 - St. DIONYSIUS (260-268)
26 - St. FELIX I (269-274)
27 - St. EUTYCHIAN (275-283)
28 - (St.) CAIUS (283-296)
29 - St. MARCELLINUS (296-304)
30 - St. MARCELLUS I (308-309)
31 - St. EUSEBIUS (309)
32 - (St.) MILTIADES (311-14)
33 - St. SYLVESTER I (314-35)
34 - St. MARK (336)
35 - St. JULIUS I (337-52)
36 - LIBERIUS (352-66)
37 - St. DAMASUS I (366-84)
38 - St. SIRICIUS (384-99)
39 - St. ANASTASIUS I (399-401)
40 - St. INNOCENT I (401-17)
41 - St. ZOSIMAS (417-18)
42 - St. BONIFACE I (418-22)
43 - St. CELESTINE I (422-32)
44 - (St.) SIXTUS III (432-40)
45 - St. LEO I (the Great) (440-61)
46 - St. HILARIUS (461-68)
47 - St. SIMPLICIUS (468-83)
48 - St. FELIX III (II) (483-92)
49 - St. GELASIUS I (492-96)
50 - (St.) ANASTASIUS II (496-98)
51 - St. SYMMACHUS (498-514)
52 - St. HORMISDAS (514-23)
53 - St. JOHN I (523-26)
54 - St. FELIX IV (III) (526-30)
55 - BONIFACE II (530-32)
56 - JOHN II (533-35)
57 - St. AGAPETUS I (535-36)
58 - St. SILVERIUS (536-37)
59 - VIGILIUS (537-55)
60 - PELAGIUS I (556-61)
61 - JOHN III (561-74)
62 - BENEDICT I (575-79)
63 - PELAGIUS II (579-90)
64 - St. GREGORY I (the Great)(590-604)
65 - SABINIAN (604-606)
66 - BONIFACE III (607)
67 - BONIFACE IV (608-15)
68 - St. ADEODATUS I (615-18)

69 - BONIFACE V (619-25)
70 - HONORIUS I (625-38)
71 - SEVERINUS (640)
72 - JOHN IV (640-42)
73 - THEODORE I (642-49)
74 - St. MARTIN I (649-55)
75 - St. EUGENE I (654-57)
76 - St. VITALIAN (657-72)
77 - ADEODATUS II (672-76)
78 - DONUS (676-78)
79 - St. AGATHO (678-81)
80 - St. LEO II (682-83)
81 - St. BENEDICT II (684-85)
82 - JOHN V (685-86)
83 - CONON (686-87)
84 - St. SERGIUS I (687-701)
85 - JOHN VI (701-05)
86 - JOHN VII (705-07)
87 - SISINNIUS (708)
88 - CONSTANTINE (708-15)
89 - St. GREGORY II (715-31)
90 - St. GREGORY III (731-41)
91 - St. ZACHARY (741-52)
92 - STEPHEN II (III) (752-57)
93 - St. PAUL I (757-67)
94 - STEPHEN III (IV) (767-72)
95 - ADRIAN I (772-95)
96 - St. LEO III (795-816)
97 - STEPHEN IV (V) (816-17)
98 - St. PASCHAL I (817-24)
99 - EUGENE II (824-27)
100 - VALENTINE (827)
101 - GREGORY IV (827-44)
102 - SERGIUS II (844-47)
103 - St. LEO IV (847-55)
104 - BENEDICT III (855-58)
105 - St. NICHOLAS I (858-67)
106 - ADRIAN II (867-72)
107 - JOHN VIII (872-82)
108 - MARINUS I (882-84)
109 - St. ADRIAN III (884-85)
110 - STEPHEN V (VI) (885-91)
111 - FORMOSUS (891-96)
112 - BONIFACE VI (896)
113 - STEPHEN VI (VII) (896-97)
114 - ROMANUS
   (August-November, 897)
115 - THEODORE II (897)
116 - JOHN IX (898-900)
117 - BENEDICT IV (900-03)
118 - LEO V (July-September, 903)
119 - SERGIUS III (904-11)
120 - ANASTASIUS III (911-13)
121 - LANDO (913-14)
122 - JOHN X (914-28)
123 - LEO VI (May-September, 928)
124 - STEPHEN VII (VIII) (929-31)
125 - JOHN XI (931-35)
126 - LEO VII (936-39)
127 - STEPHEN VIII (IX) (939-42)
128 - MARINUS II (942-46)
129 - AGAPETUS II (946-55)
130 - JOHN XII (955-63)
131 - LEO VIII (963-64)
132 - BENEDICT V (964-966)
133 - JOHN XIII (965-72)
134 - BENEDICT VI (973-74)
135 - BENEDICT VII (974-83)

136 - JOHN XIV (983-84)
137 - JOHN XV (985-96)
138 - GREGORY V (996-99)
139 - SYLVESTER II (999-1003)
140 - JOHN XVII (1003)
141 - JOHN XVIII (1003-09)
142 - SERGIUS IV (1009-12)
143 - BENEDICT VIII (1012-24)
144 - JOHN XIX (1024-32)
145-147-150- BENEDICT IX (1045)
146 - SYLVESTER III
   (January 20-February 10, 1045)
148 - GREGORY VI (1045-46)
149 - CLEMENT II (1046-47)
151 - DAMASUS II (1048)
152 - St. LEO IX (1049-54)
153 - VICTOR II (1055-57)
154 - STEPHEN IX (X) (1057-58)
155 - NICHOLAS II (1059-61)
156 - ALEXANDER II (1061-73)
157 - St. GREGORY VII (1073-85)
158 - Blessed VICTOR III (1086-87)
159 - Blessed URBAN II (1088-99)
160 - PASCHAL II (1099-1118)
161 - GELASIUS II (1118-19)
162 - CALLISTUS II (1119-24)
163 - HONORIUS II (1124-30)
164 - INNOCENT II (1130-43)
165 - CELESTINE II (1143-44)
166 - LUCIUS II (1144-45)
167 - Blessed EUGENE III (1145-53)
168 - ANASTASIUS IV (1153-54)
169 - ADRIAN IV (1154-59)
170 - ALEXANDER III (1159-81)
171 - LUCIUS III (1181-85)
172 - URBAN III (1185-87)
173 - GREGORY VIII
   (October 25- December 17, 1187)
174 - CLEMENT III (1187-91)
175 - CELESTINE III (1191-98)
176 - INNOCENT III (1198-1216)
177 - HONORIUS III (1216-27)
178 - GREGORY IX (1227-41)
179 - CELESTINE IV
   (October 28-November, 10 1241)
180 - INNOCENT IV (1243-54)
181 - ALEXANDER IV (1254-61)
182 - URBAN IV (1261-64)
183 - CLEMENT IV (1265-68)
184 - Blessed GREGORY X (1271-76)
185 - Blessed INNOCENT V (1276)
186 - ADRIAN V (1276)
187 - JOHN XXI (1276-77)
188 - NICHOLAS III (1277-80)
189 - MARTIN IV (1281-85)
190 - HONORIUS IV (1285-87)
191 - NICHOLAS IV (1288-92)
192 - St. CELESTINE V
   (July 5-December 13,1294)
193 - BONIFACE VIII (1294-1303)
194 - Blessed BENEDICT XI (1303-04)
195 - CLEMENT V (1305-14)
196 - JOHN XXII (1316-34)
197 - BENEDICT XII (1334-42)
198 - CLEMENT VI (1342-52)
199 - INNOCENT VI (1352-62)
200 - Blessed URBAN V (1362-70)
201 - GREGORY XI (1370-78)

202 - URBAN VI (1378-89)
203 - BONIFACE IX (1389-1404)
204 - INNOCENT VII (1404-06)
205 - GREGORY XII (1406-15)
206 - MARTIN V (1417-31)
207 - EUGENE IV (1431-47)
208 - NICHOLAS V (1447-55)
209 - CALLISTUS III (1455-58)
210 - PIUS II (1458-64)
211 - PAUL II (1464-71)
212 - SIXTUS IV (1471-84)
213 - INNOCENT VIII (1484-92)
214 - ALEXANDER VI (1492-1503)
215 - PIUS III (September22
   -October 18,1503)
216 - JULIUS II (1503-13)
217 - LEO X (1513-21)
218 - ADRIAN VI (1522-23)
219 - CLEMENT VII (1523-34)
220 - PAUL III (1534-49)
221 - JULIUS III (1550-55)
222 - MARCELLUS II (1555)
223 - PAUL IV (1555-59)
224 - PIUS IV (1559-65)
225 - St. PIUS V (1566-72)
226 - GREGORY XIII (1572-85)
227 - SIXTUS V (1585-90)
228 - URBAN VII (1590)
229 - GREGORY XIV (1590-91)
230 - INNOCENT IX (1591)
231 - CLEMENT VIII (1592-1605)
232 - LEO XI (1605)
233 - PAUL V (1605-21)
234 - GREGORY XV (1621-23)
235 - URBAN VIII (1623-44)
236 - INNOCENT X (1644-55)
237 - ALEXANDER VII (1655-67)
238 - CLEMENT IX (1667-69)
239 - CLEMENT X (1670-76)
240 - Blessed INNOCENT XI (1676-89)
241 - ALEXANDER VIII (1689-91)
242 - INNOCENT XII (1691-1700)
243 - CLEMENT XI (1700-21)
244 - INNOCENT XIII (1721-24)
245 - BENEDICT XIII (1724-30)
246 - CLEMENT XII (1730-40)
247 - BENEDICT XIV (1740-58)
248 - CLEMENT XIII (1758-69)
249 - CLEMENT XIV (1769-74)
250 - PIUS VI (1775-99)
251 - PIUS VII (1800-23)
252 - LEO XII (1823-29)
253 - PIUS VIII (1829-30)
254 - GREGORY XVI (1831-46)
255 - Blessed PIUS IX (1846-78)
256 - LEO XIII (1878-1903)
257 - St. PIUS X (1903-14)
258 - BENEDICT XV (1914-22)
259 - PIUS XI (1922-39)
260 - PIUS XII (1939-58)
261 - Saint JOHN XXIII (1958-63)
262 - PAUL VI (1963-78)
263 - JOHN PAUL I
   (August 26-September 28, 1978)
264 - Saint JOHN PAUL II
   (October 16, 1978-April 2, 2005)
265 - BENEDICT XVI (2005-2013)
266 - FRANCIS (March 13, 2013)

Pope Bergoglio and Pope Emeritus Ratzinger.

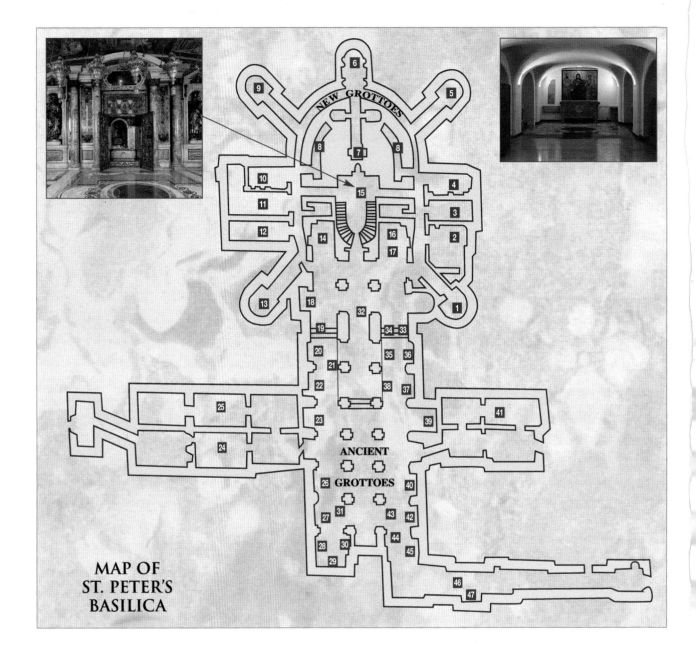

THE HOLY VATICAN GROTTOES WHERE MANY POPES LIE

1- Chapel of Saint Longin
2- Chapel of the Sainted Patrons of Europe
3- Polish Chapel
4- Irish Chapel
5- Chapel of Saint Helena
6- Tomb of Pius XII
7- Chapel of Saint Peter or Clementine
8- Semicircular crypt of Gregory the Great
9- Chapel of Veronica
10- Chapel of the "Maddonna of the Bocciata"
11- Chapel of the East
12- Chapel of Lithuania
13- Chapel of Saint Andrew
14- Mexican Chapel
15- Niche of the pallium over Saint Peter's Tomb
16- Chapel of the Orsini Madonna

17- Tomb of Pius VI
18- Tomb of Pius XI
19- Tomb of Cardinal Merry del Val
20- Tomb of the Stuarts
21- Tomb of Cardinal Frederick Todeschini
22- Tomb Innocent XIII
23- Tomb of Urban VI
24- Antiquarium Hall
25- Antiquarium Hall
26- Cenotaph of Pius III
27- Tomb of Adrian IV
28- Tomb of Gregory V
29- Tomb of Emperor Odo
30- Tomb of Julius III
31- Tomb of Mon. Ludwig Kaas
32- Altar of the Tomb

33- Tomb of Cristina of Sweden
34- Tomb of Queen Carol of Cyprus
35- Tomb of Benedict XV
36- Tomb of Innocent IX
37- Tomb of Marcellus II
38- Tomb of John Paul I
39- Tomb of Paul VI
40- Tomb of Paul II
41 - Hungarian Chapel
42- Tomb of Nicholas V
43- Tomb of Innocent VII
44- Tomb of Nicholas III
45- Tomb of Boniface VIII
46- Remains of the dividing wall of Paul III
47- Cenotaph of Callistus III